BUYING A HOME
THE SECRETS TO
BUYING AND SELLING PROPERTY

Also available

Getting the Builders in
Successful Property Letting

BUYING
A HOME

The Secrets to
Buying and Selling
Property

Paul Jager and Sue Lehmann

RIGHT WAY

Constable & Robinson Ltd
55–56 Russell Square
London WC1B 4HP
www.constablerobinson.com

First published in the UK 2004 under the title
First-Time Buyer, First-Time Seller

This new completely revised and updated edition published by
Right Way, an imprint of Constable & Robinson, 2013

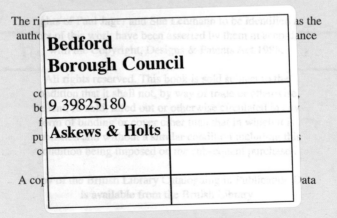

ISBN: 978-0-7160-2337-1

Printed and bound in the EU

DEDICATION

To my Mother and Father for all their support, and to
David Hughes for his help in researching this book.
Paul

To Darren, James, Daniel and Sophie Lehmann,
for always being there.
Sue

ACKNOWLEDGEMENTS

Christopher Long and David Willis.

CONTENTS

INTRODUCTION

Tullulah Bankhead, the famous Hollywood actress, once said:

"If I had to live my life again, I'd make exactly the same mistakes ... only sooner."

If only it were possible to make all our mistakes early in life. We can, though, learn from the mistakes of others, instead of committing them ourselves. This is the goal of *Buying a Home*: to help you avoid the pitfalls that others have faced when buying or selling property.

Our years of experience in the estate agency profession mean that we can share with you the secrets to successfully buying and selling property that the public rarely has access to – those tips and techniques that increase the chance of buying or selling smoothly and without stress.

Since writing the second edition, there have been various changes to the way the property market works in England and Wales. This book, therefore, provides information as at the time of writing which may alter over time; a job for the fourth edition!

The book is divided into three parts. The first tackles the subject from the purchaser's viewpoint. You'll discover how to navigate the property maze expertly, and:

- Find your perfect home.
- Successfully negotiate a sale.
- Organize the solicitor.
- Confidently resolve common problems.

The second part of the book is written for those selling property, although it is also an important read for the buyer, who needs to understand how the seller sees things. It reveals how to:

- Choose the right estate agent.
- Prepare your home for marketing.
- Deal with offers like a professional.
- Take control of your sale through to its successful conclusion.

Common to both parts are sections entitled *The Problem Clinic*. These identify common dilemmas that face buyers and sellers, and offer suggestions to resolve them.

The third part of the book details the tasks to be dealt with by both buyers and sellers between exchange and completion.

So, now, our journey begins and we start with the biggest secret of all. The one thing that above all others determines the success of buying and selling property, and that secret is... preparation.

Best of luck with the journey.

Sue and Paul

To help the text run fluently, the words 'he' or 'his' refer to both men and women. Please also note that this book discusses procedures and legal matters employed in England and Wales only as Scotland has its own method of buying and selling property.

PART ONE

THE BUYER

1

PREPARATION

The key to success when buying a property for the first time is preparation. This is a common theme throughout the book. The journey ahead of us needs thorough planning. It involves asking three fundamental questions:

- How strong is my desire to buy?
- What type of home do I need?
- What can I afford?

How Strong is My Desire to Buy?
Is your need to buy a property a definite one? At this early stage, indecision is not a problem. Asking this question later, though, after a seller has accepted your offer, will not be appreciated. If you're buying with a partner, are you both committed to ownership? Is the relationship secure enough to warrant buying a home together, which is 'life changing' (not to mention expensive)?

What Type of Home Do I Need?
There is a variety of different types of properties available to choose from. Picking the right one at the beginning will save time later. Start by listing the features your new home

must provide. Don't just think about your present needs, but consider the next two to three years. Take time over this. If necessary, ask friends and family for advice.

- Price – buyers with a tight budget will need to consider carefully how much can be 'reasonably' spent on a property.

- What accommodation is required? For those on a tight budget the accommodation on offer will be limited. Properties at the lower end of the market will probably consist of little more than a lounge, bathroom/WC, kitchen and bedroom(s). There might also be the possibility of a garden area. Studio flats are even more compact, combining the lounge, kitchen and bedroom together in one single area.

- What amenities are necessary? Do you need to be near shops and transport? Location is an important consideration. It is easier to improve a property than it is an area.

- Town or country? Living in the country may be a wonderful dream but is it practical?

- Houses are often more expensive than flats. Would it be better to buy a higher quality, larger apartment than a comparably priced but smaller house?

It is better to have the worst property in the best area than the best property in the worst area.

- What parking facilities are required? (Garages are very useful for all that junk that parents refuse to store!)

- Planning for a family? Will a flat be large enough? Will schooling be an issue?

- Is it appropriate to buy a newly built home? Initially, they require less maintenance than an older type of property. However, you may pay a premium for 'buying new'. Remember, that sparkling kitchen and beautiful bathroom will soon look worn and used. Alternatively, builders may be offering specific deals to help buyers.

- To help with the mortgage payments, would it be wise to buy a property with one more bedroom than you need? It can then be rented out and provide additional household income. (This may involve tax and mortgage implications which need to be checked.)

- Is there the time, energy, and resources to look after a house, or would a flat be more appropriate? In the next section we look at the pros and cons of each.

HOUSES
Houses are normally built over two floors and the commonest are:

- *Terraced.* A row of properties attached to each other.

- *Semi-detached.* Houses which are built in pairs.

- *Detached.* A property standing apart from others.

- *Townhouse.* The accommodation for this type of home is arranged differently from any of those defined above. It is usually built over three floors; with the lounge on the first floor, while the bedrooms are often divided over the first and second floors. The garage can be an integral part of the building, or be in a separate garage block.

- *Bungalow.* While not strictly a house, it only differs by being constructed on a single floor.

Houses are normally freehold, unlike flats which are usually leasehold, so the purchaser owns the property without any time-scale restrictions or imposed maintenance charges. This said, it is quite common for houses in the north of England to be leasehold.

Advantages of buying a house, compared to a flat:
• Greater privacy and own garden.
• Possibly less noise.
• Own front door rather than a communal entrance.
• Possibly larger accommodation.
• The opportunity to extend and alter the property in the future (subject to any restrictions).

Disadvantages of buying a house, compared to a flat:
• Generally more expensive to maintain and heat (because it has more than one floor).
• Possibly more expensive to buy.

FLATS
Flats and maisonettes are a popular choice for the first-time buyer. They can be purpose built (which means constructed for that purpose) or converted (a building which has later been changed into flats).

Although the terms 'flat' and 'maisonette' are often used interchangeably, there are strictly speaking differences between the two:

• Flats are usually one of many in a block; maisonettes can form part of a smaller building.

• Unlike a maisonette, a flat has a communal entrance before reaching its front door.

• A maisonette may have its own garden area, while a flat's tends to be communal (if it has any), i.e. for the benefit of all the residents.

For simplicity, the remainder of the book will use the term 'flat' to describe both types.

Is a Flat for Me?
For some, living in a flat is ideal.

• Those with busy lifestyles benefit from occupying a building where the maintenance is undertaken by others (the managing agent or residents' association).

   This generally includes communal gardens, repairs to the building, and external decoration.

• There is a greater feeling of security being in close proximity to others. This, though, can be a disadvantage, if noise becomes an issue.

Disadvantages include:
• Climbing flights of stairs.
• Restrictions in the lease which might, for example, prohibit pets or the erection of a satellite dish.

Compared with houses, there are three additional matters to consider with a flat:

Costs
There may be additional expenditure, i.e. ground rent, and maintenance (often called service) charge. Buyers need to allow for these in their living expenses, and be aware of any potential for changes to them in the future.

   The ground rent is usually a nominal amount, payable to the freeholder, for example, £100 per year.

   The maintenance charge, which is more applicable to flats than maisonettes, is paid towards the upkeep of the building. It can vary greatly from block to block, depending on how well they are cared for. Lifts for example are an expensive luxury, and can greatly increase the maintenance charge. Before buying a flat, confirm that no costly repairs to the building are imminent, as you will be expected to contribute; a nasty shock if you have only recently moved in!

Which Floor?

Consider the pros and cons of living on particular floors of a block. The ground floor may be more of a security risk than higher floors. However, stairs are an inconvenience when you are weighed down with shopping bags or a pushchair. This is why first-floor flats are so popular; fewer stairs to climb, and less chance of a burglar shinning up a drainpipe to your window.

The Lease

Flats and maisonettes are normally leasehold properties. This means that the owner of the building (the freeholder) grants the buyer exclusive possession of the flat for an agreed period. For example, a lease might allow 'ownership' of a flat for 99 or 125 years from 1 August 2013. When you buy this flat, the buyer will have the benefit of whatever 'ownership' time is left. Other information included in a lease concern:

a) Your responsibilities as the 'owner'.

b) Who has responsibility for other aspects of the building, for example, maintenance for such as the gardens, internal and external decoration, common areas such as halls, landings and stairways, the roof, and window cleaning, etc. This is either under the supervision of the residents' association or a third party called a 'managing agent'.

It is possible to purchase a flat, which in addition to the lease also has its share of the building's freehold. If the residents have ownership of the freehold, the advantages are:

- The duration of the leases can be extended for little charge.

- There may be little point in paying ground rent, as the party receiving it are the residents.

- It is a nice 'extra' to offer when reselling the property.

- The residents have greater control over the building.

What Can I Afford?
Most buyers need financial help to buy a property. This is normally in the form of a mortgage from a bank/building society or through an independent financial adviser. While the first provide their own specific mortgage products, the latter can recommend mortgages from many different sources.

Searching for the right mortgage can be a dizzying experience. There are so many types to choose from. They seem to change constantly and there is so much jargon to learn. Once again, a little time spent preparing will help you through this maze. Begin by asking:

- Can I afford monthly mortgage payments? This is a long-term commitment, and a regular income and strict budget plan will be needed. A financial adviser will ask that a 'Client Fact Find' form be completed to help answer this question. Remember that mortgage rates can go up as well as down, which means that your monthly mortgage payments will do the same.

- Is it appropriate to buy a home? Are your personal and financial circumstances secure enough for such a major commitment?

- Can the costs involved in running a home be met? This includes utility bills, credit card payments, food, clothes, recreation, council tax, telephone bills, inevitable repairs, building and contents insurance, travel and car expenses, and general maintenance.

SHARING THE BURDEN

With the price of property having substantially increased over the last 20 years (even allowing for recessions), climbing onto the property ladder can be a challenge. There are ways though that buyers, especially first-time buyers, who do not have the financial resources to buy a property on their own, are able to get onto the property market. Before detailing these, however, we must add a strong word of caution. None of the following options is ideal. They demand careful planning and much thought, if problems are to be avoided.

One solution is to buy a property with a friend or relation; just remember that owning property is a major undertaking and you should select your future housemate(s) with care. Draw up a legal agreement between all the parties involved so that each knows what will happen if/when one of you decides it is time to move on. Records of exact details of how much each of you has contributed towards the deposit and mortgage, and other household expenses, also need to be kept.

Lastly, it is important that everyone genuinely understands the commitment they are about to make. A mortgage needs to be paid regularly, as do any outgoings. Confirming that those involved with the purchase are able to make this ongoing financial commitment is vital, before exchange of contracts. Additional money will also be needed for those incidentals that unexpectedly occur. A leaking gutter, or broken washing machine needs to be allowed for. Having a separate bank account where everyone pays in an agreed amount every month should provide a reserve of money for just such occurrences.

Some people, who do not have a friend or relation who is willing to buy a property with them, use one of the co-buying websites now set up on the internet to find someone to share with. However, there are serious security and financial implications that need to be considered for anyone going down this route. We ourselves would not feel comfortable entering into such an important relationship with a stranger, although others may feel differently.

A far less risky solution is to find a shared ownership scheme run by the government (HomeBuy) or a local housing association. Shared ownership enables you to buy a certain percentage of the property, and then to pay rent on the proportion you don't yet own. There are various schemes available for key workers and first-time buyers, including one which helps those wishing to buy a new property, and another which helps tenants who want to buy a share in the home they already rent. Check out the latest information on the government website *www.gov.uk* and contact your local housing association.

THE MORTGAGE

Since the first and second editions of this book were published, the mortgage landscape has changed out of all recognition. At the time of writing, it is now quite a challenge to obtain a mortgage and the requirements necessary are constantly changing. Therefore it is not appropriate to offer definitive information on mortgages here. We would suggest instead that you take advice from such people as qualified financial advisers or mortgage lenders.

THE DEPOSIT

Although mortgages for the entire purchase price may be available, it is customary to buy a property with a mixture of mortgage and a buyer's own money. The latter is called the 'deposit'. For example, if a mortgage of £90,000 is being borrowed, and the buyer has £10,000 savings, a home of £100,000 can be bought (assuming you have additional money to set aside for other moving expenses, such as for solicitors, stamp duty, removals, etc. – see below).

Even at this early stage, it is important to confirm that:

• The deposit is definitely available, particularly if being provided by family or friends.

- There are no delays obtaining the deposit. For example, do shares need to be sold or is the money being transferred from abroad? This will affect the timescale of any offer you make.

ADDITIONAL COSTS
There is much to consider when buying a first home, so it is easy to overlook other associated expenses.

1. Stamp duty, correctly referred to as stamp duty land tax. This is a government tax, paid by the purchaser once the property has been bought. The amount is dependent on the sale price. (The rates and thresholds given below are correct at the time of going to press, but can be changed by the Chancellor of the Exchequer at any time, so you should check the up-to-date position.)

   Up to and including £125,000 – Nothing payable.

   £125,001 to and including £250,000 – 1 per cent of the entire price of the property.

   £250,001 to and including £500,000 – 3 per cent of the entire price of the property.

   £500,001 to and including £1,000,000 – 4 per cent of the entire price of the property.

   £1,000,001 to and including £2,000,000 – 5 per cent of the entire price of the property.

   Over £2,000,000 – 7 per cent of the entire price of the property.

   Over £2,000,000 and bought through a company – 15 per cent (from 22 March 2012).

2. Survey fees.

3. Land Registry fee (registering the property in the new owner's name).

4. Unexpected costs, for example, additional surveys if defects are found.

5. Removal costs.

6. Household items.

7. Buildings insurance (put in place from 'exchange of contracts', to cover the property for damage, fire, subsidence, etc.). It may be worth enquiring whether there are any incentives for taking buildings insurance from the same company that is lending you the mortgage.

8. Are penalties incurred if the mortgage is paid off early? Is there an 'arrangement fee' associated with taking a particular mortgage scheme? What may initially seem a very attractive mortgage deal might seem less appealing when it comes to paying this additional cost.

9. Abortive sale (the buyer or seller decides not to proceed). In this situation, costs already incurred may be lost, such as survey fee, solicitor's fees, and mortgage arrangement fee.

10. Your solicitor at 'exchange of contracts' will need 5 per cent to 10 per cent of the purchase price. This is a non-returnable deposit. (Those taking a 100 per cent mortgage will need to make alternative arrangements with their solicitor, as mentioned above.)

11. Solicitors' fee. This is worthy of further explanation. In order to buy a property, ownership needs to be transferred to the purchaser, using legal documents and procedures. This is called 'conveyancing' and is undertaken by a solicitor (or legal executive, or licensed conveyancer).

    The difference between a solicitor, legal executive and licensed conveyancer is one of experience and qualification. All three are able to deal competently with the conveyancing process.

    However, the solicitor has a broader range of legal knowledge and can therefore deal with any other law related matters, such as wills, while the licensed conveyancer is only qualified to deal with the conveyancing procedure itself. The term 'solicitor' is used for the remainder of the book to denote all three types of conveyancer.

    When choosing a solicitor, pick one who has the time and patience to guide you through the process. These are qualities worth paying for (and we would always advocate using a solicitor rather than attempting the legal work yourself).

    Their fee can be based on either an hourly rate or a single amount for the entire transaction. Choose two or three solicitors and compare their charges and service before making a decision. Confirm the cost of the 'total' package, whether the fee includes any additional costs (for legal documents such as searches), and if there is a charge for an abortive sale.

    Having made your choice, confirm that you want to use their services, and will call again when a property has been found; it is premature to incur any expenses at this stage.

2

LOOKING FOR PROPERTY

The preparation is complete. Now the most exciting part of our journey begins: searching for our dream home.

The Estate Agent

The most popular and successful method of finding properties for sale is through estate agents. Their reputation may have been tarnished over the years, but they still offer the best access to the vast majority of properties for sale in England and Wales.

Competition for property can be fierce with far more people (called 'applicants' or 'buyers') wanting to buy than there are homes for sale. This is particularly true in an active property market. An agent might be marketing 20 flats, but hold information on over 200 flat seekers. Even with such technology as text messaging and emails, it is not always possible for the agent to contact all these people simultaneously each time a flat comes to the market. There will always be some who, through chance alone, are lucky enough to be informed first. They now have the opportunity to make an offer before anyone else! However, this limitation of the system can work in the educated buyer's favour.

TAKING ADVANTAGE OF THE SYSTEM

Successful estate agents will always keep a select list of applicants interested in specific types of property. These are people who the agent believes are keen to buy immediately (so bringing him closer to a sale and his monthly commission cheque). They are termed 'hot prospects', and immediately contacted when a suitable property becomes available. How can you become one of this elite number?

- You have already fulfilled the first requirement by following the advice in the previous chapter: being prepared. This demonstrates to the agent that you have taken this matter seriously.

- Prove you are a keen buyer by being enthusiastic and ready to view properties at every opportunity.

- Follow the instructions in this chapter!

YOUR VITAL STATISTICS

Leave your property requirements with as many estate agents as possible. If you can, visit rather than telephone or email (personal contact increases the chance of being remembered).

The agent will start by asking for name, address and contact details. Leave plenty of these; how unfortunate would it be to miss the ideal property because the agent only had your work telephone number? If the estate agent is technologically savvy he may also be able to email or send a text message, with details of homes for sale. This is becoming increasingly common.

After noting your price range and property requirements, the agent will then ask three very important questions. The answers will brand you as either 'Mr Average' buyer or a 'hot prospect' worthy of special attention:

- When do you want to buy?

- When can you view?

- Do you have a property to sell?

'Now'
'Now', and
if you are a first-time buyer you can state that you are 'ready to purchase a property immediately'.

Lastly, they may offer free mortgage advice from the agency's in-house financial adviser. Take advantage of this. There is no obligation, and ideas might be suggested which you hadn't considered before; seize any opportunity to learn from those in the know.

PROPERTY DETAILS
Having matched your requirements to the agency's properties, you'll be given the appropriate property information. If, in the past, estate agents were renowned for pushing poetic licence to its limits, the 1991 Property Misdescriptions Act (PMA) now ensures all material has to be factual and honest. No longer does the phrase 'situated within a five minute walk of the shops' mean 'but only for those blessed with the lightning speed of an Olympic sprinter'. Even the photographs have to conform to the PMA and accurately reflect the true nature of a property. If, however, anything remains unclear, ask further questions such as:

- Is the property situated on a main road?

- What lies at the rear of the garden?

- How old is the maisonette?

• How many flats are there in the block?

• (If unclear from the photograph) What lies either side of the property?

You may also find that agents supply details on homes in excess of your budget. They assume that:

• The owner may consider an offer from a buyer, if his aim is to move quickly.

• The buyer may pay a little more for the ideal property.

These are reasonable assumptions. A buyer should also remain open-minded when studying the details, as properties that may initially seem unsuitable could be altered to fulfil his needs. For example:

• The spacious flat with panoramic views, but the awful 1960s kitchen and poor decoration. The latter can easily be rectified over time (funds permitting).

• That perfect two-bedroom cottage, which has a through lounge when two rooms were wanted. Could this lounge be partitioned into two (subject to regulations)?

• For a first home, how much of a real disadvantage is it to have a maisonette with an electric heating system instead of a gas one?

Never compromise your standards, just stay aware of a home's potential.

YOUR BEST FRIEND – THE ESTATE AGENT
To increase the chance of becoming a 'hot prospect', strike up a personal rapport with the estate agent. Agents are accustomed

to apathy and defensiveness from the public. Be different. Take an interest in them. They are more likely to do business with someone they like and feel comfortable with, rather than an applicant who treats them like just another salesman. Keep in regular contact so that you are at the forefront of their minds when that beautiful home becomes available.

This is one of the reasons why technology is unlikely to replace the high street estate agent any time soon. Contact between the public and agent is a vital element in the business relationship. While it is perfectly possible to access most companies' properties for sale online, the interaction between you and them is lost if your only contact is via their website. We would suggest therefore that regardless of being able to download property details or send the organization your requirements by email, you also make an effort to contact them by phone or better still visit. There is infinitely more chance of them remembering you and, more importantly, your needs.

The Auction Room
Purchasing a property at auction is an option that a buyer should be wary of. It may be important to question why the owner (or person in charge of the property) has decided to go to auction, rather than use an estate agent. It is possible that the property has a problem, i.e. structural defects or is in need of renovation, which would have made a sale on the open market very difficult. This may result in the property being sold at a discounted price, but you must consider how much any work will cost, and how much effort would be required in finding willing tradesmen to complete the work. You must also bear in mind that a lender may not be happy to provide a mortgage on this type of property, with the risks involved.

Clearly, a lot of research must be undertaken before a buyer even considers bidding for such a property.

The method of sale at an auction is entirely different from that of an estate agent, although it does initially involve viewing the property for sale.

- The 'offer' is made in an auction room, in the company of other interested parties, at a specified date and time.

- A price guide may not be available, although there will be a 'reserve' figure set by the owner, beneath which he will not sell. The bidder offering the highest price above the reserve will be successful.

- Once a bid has been accepted, an exchange of contracts is immediate. Consequently, all legal, financial and survey enquiries will need to be completed by the buyer prior to the auction taking place. The mortgage must be in place, and a deposit available.

There are also two further matters which must be considered:

- Keep to an agreed budget and do not allow the enthusiasm and competition of other bidders to encourage you to exceed this limit.

- Money will need to be spent on surveys, solicitors, etc., even if your bid is ultimately unsuccessful.

The Internet
As has been mentioned, most estate agencies now have their own websites. It is the equivalent of a virtual shop front, open 24 hours a day. For the buyer this is an ideal place to visit. It provides the opportunity to investigate an area without the cost and effort of travelling. It may also offer the chance to send your property requirements to the company by email. However, to make the point again, use this service but also telephone and visit if possible; remember there is no substitute for personal contact.

Also, there are shortcomings to these websites:

- If managed by a third party, property details can be out of date, and properties offered may already be sold subject to contract.

- Finding sites among the millions of pages in cyberspace can be difficult unless you know the company's web address. Use a search engine such as Google or Yahoo. Look for the website addresses in agents' local newspaper advertisements or on 'For Sale' boards. Internet portals (virtual warehouses containing information and web addresses on sites in specific subject areas) are a good source of information. They include such sites as *www.rightmove.co.uk* and *www. email4property.co.uk.*

Private Sales
Buying a property directly from the owner without using estate agents is a further option.

On the plus side
- The owner may reduce the price of his property because he has saved paying commission.

- Direct contact with the owner may appeal to a purchaser who doesn't like dealing through intermediaries.

On the down side
- There is no estate agent to advise you during the sale.

- Should problems occur there is no intermediary, and you will need to confront the owner yourself.

Private sales are advertised in several ways:

- Advertisements in the classified section of local newspapers.

- Advertising in local shop windows.

- Creating a website with details and pictures of the property for sale.

- A home-made 'For Sale' board erected outside the property.

Use Your Initiative – Find the Ideal Home by Yourself
Some years ago, Paul decided to move from suburbia and relocate to the country. Unfortunately, there was very little for sale in the areas he wanted, and competition was fierce for the few houses available. With his own flat under offer, time was against him. Each week he contacted the local estate agents and scanned the newspapers, but with no success. Eventually he realized he couldn't rely on these options, and a more creative approach was needed. He picked four roads, in an area he liked, and hand delivered leaflets. These were very simple and created on his computer.

The wording read:

'I apologize for contacting you in this fashion but I am keen to move into your area. Unfortunately, there is little for sale at the moment. If you had considered moving I would be very happy to hear from you.

I should also add that I am a private individual and not an estate agent seeking business.

I look forward to hearing from you.'

Delivering them was an opportunity to find any 'For Sale' boards that had just appeared. It also helped increase Paul's knowledge of the area, and discover any hidden cul-de-sac of homes he hadn't noticed before.

His next step would have been to visit local shops and public houses to 'spread the word' that he wanted to move into the village. Word of mouth can be a very powerful tool in closely knit communities. He had also intended to place an advertisement in the local newspaper's classified section (a shorter version of the leaflet). Its aim was to unearth homes that were soon to be for sale. However, he found a property before receiving any responses.

'If you want something done then do it yourself' is the lesson learnt here.

Conclusion – The Savvy Buyer

Whether following the traditional route of visiting estate agents or taking advantage of technology and the internet, there are plenty of places to search for properties for sale. It just takes perseverance. Set aside time, once a week, to check websites and call agents. Deliver leaflets and stay aware of what is happening in your chosen area. This will put you 'head and shoulders' above most other buyers who are content to sit and wait to be contacted.

3

THE APPOINTMENT

Television programmes about selling property have become increasingly popular; people have a fascination with other people's homes. This is no surprise to estate agents; they've known for years that the public enjoys visiting properties and seeing how others live. For some buyers, though, it can be a daunting experience; what questions to ask the owners, what features to look for, how inquisitive can you reasonably be? This is our next topic.

Arranging the Appointment
BEING SELECTIVE
After the previous chapter, you probably have an avalanche of property details. Divide these into three groups:

- Those that seem suitable.
- Those that leave you undecided.
- Those that fail to meet the criteria.

The list of requirements, made in the preparation stage, will be useful. The most important factors were probably:

- Price.
- Location.
- Room size.
- Accommodation.

Followed by:
- Condition.
- Special features (i.e. fireplaces, period features, garden).

And for flats:
- Length of the lease.
- Charges involved (for example, service charge and ground rent).

The 'seems suitable' category is our first priority. View these immediately. Next, are there any in the 'undecided' group worthy of re-consideration? As discussed earlier, stay open-minded. As for the last category, 'unsuitable homes', keep these; they are useful as a guide to property prices in the area.

BOOKING THE APPOINTMENT
Organize only three or four appointments to view properties in a day. Any more and eyes glaze over, concentration wanes and the process becomes tiring. To aid the memory, take notes (but ask the owner's permission).

Be selective about the viewing times. Avoid the dark. It can conceal a multitude of sins such as a shabby exterior, a poor looking roof, etc.

If the property is on a main road, then visit during rush hour to check the noise level. Noise considerations at different times of day also apply to properties near schools, public houses, noisy factories or plant, dog kennels, aerodromes and places of worship. Be very careful about proximity to railway lines or busy airport flight paths. Lastly choose times when neighbours are at home, to gauge the available parking, and noise levels. This is certainly true if buying a flat in a block (although a quiet neighbour today can be replaced by a 'neighbour from hell' tomorrow).

All appointments are organized through the estate agent. Use the opportunity to ask this agent about the circumstances surrounding the sale (which will help later when making an offer):

- Are they the only agency marketing the property? If not, perhaps this suggests that the owner is keen to sell.

- How long has the property been on the market? If many months, maybe the owner will consider an offer?

- Is the property still for sale? Imagine walking around that 'perfect' home only to be told by the owners that they accepted an offer two days ago. It is worth bearing in mind that an estate agency is required to be a member of The Property Ombudsman or Ombudsman Services: Property. Therefore they must inform a buyer if an offer has been accepted on the property they are about to arrange a viewing for.

- Have any previous sales fallen through after survey? If so, why? Although there is no obligation on the agent to reveal this information, there is no harm in asking. If there is a 'defect', better to know now.

Other aspects of viewing:

- Security. Avoid viewing alone (or at the very least make sure someone knows where you are). Keep a mobile phone handy.

- Do not expect an estate agent to drive you to appointments; have your own transport.

- Be on time for an appointment, or ring if delayed. (If this is after office hours, ask the agent for the owner's home telephone number.)

- Unless time is very tight, avoid initially viewing properties 'from the outside', as it is just too difficult to judge the size and quality of a home from its exterior.

The Viewing

There are five elements to a successful viewing, and the clever buyer will exploit them all to help make a decision on the suitability of the property:

   a) Superficially, does the property meet your requirements?

   b) Ask the right questions of the homeowner.

   c) Are there indications of defects at the property?

   d) Is the area suitable?

   e) Never rely on a single visit.

(A) MEETING YOUR REQUIREMENTS

This needs little explanation. Your first priority is to confirm that the property's accommodation, layout and condition are satisfactory. However, as discussed before, keep these requirements flexible. This is particularly true when it comes to considering 'condition'. Always look beyond the superficial. A dirty or poorly kept home, for example, can be transformed with only a minimum of effort. It is possible to buy a property at a reasonable price which has been dismissed by others simply because of its poor presentation. Also be mindful that a beautifully decorated home, which is probably highly priced, will quickly lose its glamour with wear and tear. It may also be concealing problems behind its alluring façade.

(B) QUESTIONS

Some years ago, we met a couple who had bought a property, and then discovered it had subsidence (a structural defect, caused by movement, which can manifest itself as cracking in the walls). They only noticed this after moving in and opening wardrobe doors in the main bedroom for the first time. The wardrobes had no backs, and cracks were visible in the wall behind. This alerted them to a problem, which ultimately proved to be serious. The property had structural defects, resolved only by relying on an insurance claim, creating a lot of stress and worry for the couple. If the couple had checked the wardrobes properly in the first place, they would have discovered the problem right at the start.

> *Never be afraid to ask questions of the owner or seek permission to investigate something in more detail.*

- Is the garage large enough for your car?

- What are the neighbours like?

- Are there receipts and current guarantees for work undertaken at the property, i.e. for a damp course, electrical wiring, extensions, etc.?

- How long has the property been on the market?

- Has the property been surveyed recently and if so were any problems highlighted?

- Why is the owner moving?

- When does the owner want to move?

- Are there any defects to the property or outstanding insurance claims you need to be aware of?

- Is there any unfinished work to be completed?

- What fixtures are being taken, including those in the garden, like plants or the shed?

- Are the ground rent and maintenance payments (for a flat) up to date?

- Are there any major works planned or heavy expenditure expected (at a block of flats)?

This is also a good chance to raise the subject of building construction. Properties are built in a number of ways, including steel framed, timber framed, brick and block, and concrete. For example, while many homes have external walls of brick and then a second lining of concrete block, others employ a timber frame to support the building.

Often it is difficult from appearance alone to tell which of these has been used. Information from the owner, estate agent or surveyor will be needed. It is important to obtain this, as these materials can have a direct influence on the price paid, ability to obtain a mortgage, and resaleability. Some mortgage lenders, for example, may decline to lend on a particular type of construction. Because this will leave the property with a more 'minority appeal', its asking price should be lower and reselling it later may prove difficult. Unfortunately, a book of this size cannot do this subject justice, and it is one better dealt with by further research or a conversation with a surveyor, estate agent or financial adviser.

(c) PLAYING SHERLOCK HOLMES – INDICATIONS OF DEFECTS
It is said that 'a little knowledge can be a dangerous thing'. This section therefore needs to be read with great caution. It is a very basic guide and certainly not exhaustive as to signs of possible defects in a property. Keep them in mind during your visit. Ask the surveyor to investigate further should the sale be pursued.

1. The walk to the front door offers the first indication of a property's condition.

- Window frames. Are they in need of repair or replacing? Has double glazing been installed? (Inspect windows carefully as some modern single glazed windows look 'double glazed'.)

- Do the roof and chimney look in reasonable condition? A pair of binoculars will help identify whether any tiles are missing or have slipped. If the roof is beginning to 'show its age' then it may be necessary to renew it completely rather than just 'paper over the cracks' by repairing it. With the binoculars to hand also examine the guttering. Is it the modern plastic variety, or older metal type? Are there signs of leaking, suggesting poor condition, or a blockage from things such as leaves, that needs investigation?

- Are there cracks in the walls? This might be the sign of structural defects (such as subsidence) and will demand further investigation by a qualified surveyor. It can be caused by close proximity to a large tree whose roots are extracting excessive amounts of water from the ground. As the moisture content of the ground changes, this can destabilize the building or parts of it and cause 'movement'. New properties, though, may also have cracking, but probably because a newly built home takes time to 'bed down' into its surroundings. It is remedied by the builder repairing the cracks (a process called 'snagging').

- What is the condition of the brickwork, and the mortar binding it? Although it is only a minor item, employing a professional to 'repoint' because the mortar is disintegrating can be a costly exercise.

2. As you walk around the building do the floors feel springy? This could be the effect of 'dry rot', a fungus that affects timbers. It can travel throughout a building and may require major remedial work to resolve. Its companion, however, 'wet rot' is less of an issue. It causes timbers to become brittle, but can be halted if the affected areas are replaced. There are numerous companies dealing with woodworm and damp matters that provide advice on this subject.

3. Stains on walls suggest:

   • Damp penetrating through from the exterior due to per-haps leaking guttering or a failing 'flat roof' (a cheaper form of roofing often found in properties that have been extended).

   • A previous (or ongoing) leak from water pipes above.

We visited a home that the owners were keen to sell. They had described it as a four-bedroom property. However we discovered that the fourth bedroom was reached by climbing a ladder into the loft. Although when we reached it the room itself was beautifully decorated, it could not have had the necessary building regulations demanded by the local council; a lack of a standard staircase was a clue. The owners also confirmed this. Consequently, under estate agency law, it could not be classed as a four-bedroom house, but instead a three-bedroom one. The fourth bedroom was not lawful or legitimate, and the price was lowered accordingly. Buyers beware of similar situations. If in doubt, quiz the selling agent or owner to evidence all necessary written permissions for a particular construction.

   • Condensation. Often occurs in bathrooms with poor ventilation.

• Moisture may be penetrating the interior at ground level, as rising damp. This can be both visible or as an odour. A new damp course (a membrane that acts as a barrier to the moisture) will remedy this.

4. While walking around a room or hallway does it feel as if the floor is uneven or sloping to one side? Do the interior doors close properly and are the frames around them square? If not, then this could be a structural defect, i.e. the home is 'moving' and will definitely need further investigation. Without insulting the homeowner, politely ask him about this. If he is aware of such structural problems, then you may consider avoiding this home, even if an insurance claim is pending.

5. How old is the central heating boiler? Does it look worn and battered? Does any of its exterior look corroded? If so, it could be coming to the end of its life. Even if all seems well, exterior appearances can be deceptive. Ask whether the boiler is regularly serviced, and have this confirmed by your solicitor and surveyor. During the winter months, ask to see the boiler actually working, including the timer if it has one. Check also that the radiators heat up properly.

6. Has the property been altered in any way, and if so were the necessary permissions obtained (building regulations and/or planning permissions) for such as the following?

   (a) An adjoining lounge and dining room which have been combined into one through-lounge.

   (b) Rooms that have been built into the loft.

   (c) Extensions.

   (d) The removal of chimney breasts.

7. What are the water pipes made of? Lead is now frowned
    upon for health reasons.

8. Are there any artexed ceilings (or other roof coverings)
    which might contain asbestos fibres, which have health
    implications? The same could be true, for example, for
    certain garage roof coverings. These matters will need
    advice from a surveyor.

9. Are there streams or rivers close by that may lead to
    flooding?

10. What condition are the boundary fences in? If in need of
    repair who is responsible for them?

11. While not a 'defect', ask whether anyone has rights over the
    property i.e. restrictive covenants and easements. These are
    legal matters but ones that a buyer should be aware of. The
    first is a restriction placed on the property to stop something
    being done with it. For example, a restrictive covenant
    might be that the building cannot be used as a place of
    work, or cannot be altered in some way. The second type,
    the easement, is a right that someone has over your land.

12. Again, not a defect, but ask whether there are any shared drains
    on the property and who is responsible for their upkeep.

---

*Some years ago Paul was considering buying a cottage
until he noticed gates at the end of the garden. These
were to allow the neighbours to enter his garden
trundling their wheelie bins behind them to reach
an access road at the end of the row of houses from
where the binmen collected the refuse each week.
This is called a 'right of way' and may affect the
price of the property (and certainly affected Paul's
decision to buy it!).*

(D) BEYOND THE FRONT DOOR

Buying a home involves not only its suitability, but also that of the area around it. Investigate the surrounding roads, and be mindful of:

• Noisy children in the road that might disturb you if you are a shift worker.

• Burnt out cars or boarded shop fronts that suggest a problem area.

• Parking restrictions.

• How well are the communal areas of a block of flats maintained?

Reading local newspapers can also provide clues to an area, and help us make a more informed decision about buying our first home.

(E) REFRESHING THE MEMORY – NEVER RELY ON A SINGLE VISIT

Before making a decision about the property, arrange a second visit (unless there are already other interested parties, and time is against you). There are certain to be features you failed to notice the first time, for example:

• Is that second bedroom really large enough?

• Didn't the kitchen seem bigger the first time?

• Are there more steps to this second-floor flat than you remember?

• How close is the property to that school playground?

• Does the flat have loft space?

Use this opportunity for all parties involved with the purchase, or who have a financial interest, to see the property. If, for example, a couple are buying their home, then both need to see it. This is too important a matter for decisions to be made on someone else's behalf. Before a final decision is made, an internal inspection by all parties involved is a necessity.

4

THE OFFER

Having decided on the right property, the next step is to make an offer. The main difficulty at this stage is deciding on an offer price which is both affordable for the buyer and an acceptable figure for the seller. Feelings of tension surface, excitement levels rise, there is a tangible sense of anticipation in the air... and this is just the reaction of the estate agent! The offer process is divided into four sections:

• Preparation.
• The offer.
• Negotiation.
• Acceptance.

Preparation
The law in this country is far from perfect when it comes to buying a residential property. A buyer or seller can withdraw at any time and for any reason prior to 'exchange of contracts'. This is a devastating experience, and is often due to lack of preparation. Problems occur that should have been addressed at the start, if the relevant groundwork had been done. The following questions will help.

ASK YOURSELF:
• *Do we need to see the property again before making an offer?*
Would it help to arrange a further visit with someone who can provide an unbiased opinion?

If there are future plans to alter the property structurally, take a builder with you for advice (having asked the owner's permission).

• *Has the area around the property been investigated thoroughly?*
Travel to the property using different routes, and at different times of the day and week, to highlight any features that may not have been obvious before.

• *Speak to the police about the level of crime in the area and 'neighbourhood watch' schemes.*
Read the local papers for a few weeks if you live some distance away, to get an idea of the local 'culture'.

• *Ask the local council for information.*
Is this a conservation area and subject to building restrictions? Are there proposed developments nearby or changes in transport/shopping facilities that may affect the price in the future? (Although a solicitor will investigate these matters later, it's better to ask now before making an offer.) If the reason for buying the property is to take advantage of a school's catchment area, is this guaranteed by moving to the property?

ASK THE OWNER:
• *The offer figure.*
Ask the owner for guidance on an acceptable offer – this will give you an idea of whether the offer you have in mind is a realistic one. (There is a good chance he will refuse, but it is worth a try. You might find the selling agent more amenable.)

• *What does the asking price include?*
Carpets and curtains normally remain but, if not, then budget
for them in the offer.

• *Does he know the history of the property?*
Is it a purpose built three-bedroom house or actually a two-
bedroom property which has been extended? If so, ensure that
the legal documents, such as the Planning Permission and
Building Control (Regulations) Approval, are available for this
building work.

• *Will the owner sell, regardless of finding another property
to buy?*
Will he move into rented accommodation, or do you need to
wait for him to find a property to buy? How long will this
take?

• *Has the seller already found a property to buy?*
If so, is there a 'chain' and how many others are involved?
A 'chain' means that the buyer is reliant not only on his own
purchase, but on the purchases of several others. It takes only
one of these to fail for the chain to collapse like a pack of
cards. Once you know whether there is a chain, and its length,
you can assess the level of risk involved and make an informed
decision about whether to progress.

ASK THE ESTATE AGENT:
• *How long has the property been on the market?*
If it's longer than a couple of months, the owner may well
consider an offer (especially if he has already found another
home to buy).

• *Is there more than one estate agent marketing the property?*
If so, this could suggest that the owner is keen to sell and may
accept an offer.

• *Is there anything detrimental to the property that you need to be made aware of?* For example:

1. Does anyone else have rights over the land (called easements and covenants)?

2. Has planning permission (for example, for an extension) ever been refused?

3. Has anyone previously withdrawn from buying the property and, if so, why? If a sale has failed due to a poor survey, then why waste your own time and money?

4. Have there been insurance claims for subsidence or flooding?

5. What utilities does the property offer? Some blocks of flats have no gas supply and rely wholly on electricity.

6. When buying a home on a newly built estate, will any of the other houses be sold to housing associations? This could diminish the saleability of the property in the future.

7. With a flat, what type of residents live in the block? While this can change continually, are some of the flats council owned, or managed by a housing association? Will this devalue your home?

OTHER CONSIDERATIONS
As discussed on page 22, stamp duty land tax can add considerably to the cost of buying a home. Properties above £125,000 but below £250,001 are currently liable for a 1 per cent government tax on the whole amount, while this increases to 3 per cent for those between £250,001 and £500,000.

Take the example of a property priced at £260,000. An offer of £255,000 would incur 3 per cent stamp duty at £7,650 (3% x £255,000). However, agree a sale at £249,000 and the stamp duty is decreased to 1 per cent, i.e. £2,490 (1% x £249,000). (Please note that these percentages are used as an example; rates and thresholds are subject to change.)

In this particular situation, if the owner is adamant that only £252,000 would be acceptable, then perhaps a figure of £250,000 could be agreed. The extra £2,000 would account for 'fixtures and fittings', i.e. carpets and curtains. Fixtures and fittings are not subject to stamp duty, therefore this would reduce the 3 per cent stamp duty to 1 per cent. However, this is only possible if this amount is deemed to be reasonable by HM Revenue & Customs. To confirm this, a form needs to be completed by the buyer regarding stamp duty. The Land Transaction Return ensures that unacceptable amounts are not being allocated to 'fixtures and fittings' in order to deprive the state of its revenue.

Once completed, the form is then scrutinized by HMRC to confirm that the correct amount of stamp duty has been paid, and not avoided by overstating the value of fixtures and fittings in order to bring the sale price into a lower stamp duty bracket. It is a lengthy eight pages, and will probably be completed by the buyer's solicitor (if asked nicely!) and then signed by the buyer. Information required will include details regarding the property, stamp duty amount and purchaser.

If in any doubt about how much can be allocated to fixtures and fittings, consult your solicitor.

The Offer

The estate agent will need approximately 10–15 minutes with you to go through the 'offer taking' process. His task is to:

• Present the owner with the maximum amount of relevant information about a potential purchaser.

• Ensure all circumstances surrounding this potential buyer's offer are known, in order to diminish the risk of any problems occurring later in the sale.

QUESTIONS ASKED
These will include:

Contact Details
Provide as much information as possible, in case you're needed urgently during the sale.

Has everyone involved in the sale seen the property?

Is there anyone else who needs to view the property before the offer can be made?

When do you want to move?

Do your timescales match those of the owners? For example:

• If you live in rented accommodation and need to give a period of notice (although it is too early to alert your landlord).

• If you are not a first-time buyer and need to sell your own property, what are the chain details? Do you have a buyer, who in turn is 'under offer' and the chain is complete, down to a first-time buyer?

• If holidays are planned.

Do you have a connection with anyone at the estate agents?
In order to comply with the 1979 Estate Agents Act the agent will need to know if you are a relative or connected with any member of staff at the agency.

The Amount
Come prepared with a figure. Plucking one out of thin air will not instil confidence in the agent or owner! Deciding on a figure is a balancing act between wanting to buy for the cheapest price and not wanting to insult the owner with an

embarrassingly low figure. Being aware of prices in the area will help, as will some of the questions discussed previously:

- Are other parties interested in the property?
Although the estate agent is working on behalf of his client (the homeowner) and may be tempted to suggest that a property has proved more popular than it actually has, the Estate Agents Act states that it is unlawful for the agent to suggest that there are other offers when this is untrue. However, if a property is being marketed by multiple agents, your agent may be unaware of offers being submitted through other companies.

- Has the property been on the market for some time?

- Have the owners found another home to buy?

Whatever the offer, leave yourself room to negotiate further. If the property market is falling, then this is reason enough to ensure that the price paid is as realistic as possible. However, there are circumstances when it is wise to offer as much as possible immediately:

- When other parties are interested.

- When the property market is rising quickly. Losing this home might mean having to pay a higher price for a similar one in the near future.

The goal is to make an offer attractive enough to persuade the owner to accept immediately and to refuse to deal with any other buyers. To reduce the possibility of heartache later, ask that the property be removed from the market if a sale is agreed. If refused, suggest marketing ceases for four weeks (allowing enough time for you to prove your sincerity), and persuade the seller to stop marketing once this 'trial' period is

over. If this too is unacceptable to the owner, are you prepared
to continue with the purchase knowing that the property is still
on the market?

The Financial Details
The agent will need information regarding your mortgage
requirements or financial arrangements. The more details you
supply, the more appealing your offer will be.

Having made an offer, the agent is obliged to inform the
owner in writing (and will probably do so verbally, to speed
up the process). It is an unwritten rule that offers are made
on properties one at a time. On the few occasions we dealt
with buyers who offered on several properties simultaneously,
it suggested that they were not committed to any of them and
had little consideration for anyone but themselves. Not an im-
age that will endear you to homeowners or estate agents.

Negotiation

If you are a first-time buyer, or you have nothing to sell, you are
in a strong position: no chain and able to offer an immediate
sale. Otherwise you would generally need to have your own
property 'under offer' with a completed chain. If a homeowner
doesn't accept your first offer, then ask the estate agent what
figure the seller is expecting. If the agent is not willing to
commit himself, then either:

• Offer the best figure you can afford.

Or:

• Offer a little more and gauge the reaction (remembering the
  philosophy: the longer the negotiation, the less chance of
  success).

If negotiations become protracted, but the desire to purchase
is still strong then:

- Suggest a final figure, asking that certain 'fixtures and fittings' be included; for example, curtains, free standing wardrobes, etc. Or:

- Look at the possibility of increasing the mortgage or deposit to bridge the gap. Think carefully, and beware of being swept along in the excitement of the moment. Buying a property means making regular monthly mortgage payments and not becoming overstretched financially. If necessary, arrange another appointment to confirm that this property really does warrant another offer.

If having followed these suggestions an agreement is still no closer, consider withdrawing. Life is too short to endure the stress brought on by long negotiations. Your time and energy could be better spent finding another home.

It is also worth remembering that estate agents are members of The Property Ombudsman (TPO)or Ombudsman Services: Property (OSP), thus they must confirm any offer to you and the seller in writing.

GAZUMPING

One of the major flaws in the English and Welsh property system is the ability to 'gazump'. Common in a rising market, gazumping occurs when a sale is agreed, but another person then offers a higher figure, which is accepted instead. The original buyer not only loses the property, but also any money already spent on the transaction (for example, for solicitors, surveyors, etc.).

Although some have tried, no one has yet devised a foolproof way to eradicate this. Asking for the property to be withdrawn from the market, once a sale has been agreed, can help (but still doesn't eliminate the possibility of a person who viewed the property weeks ago suddenly re-appearing and wanting to purchase it). A buyer can only hope that the homeowner has sincere intentions to sell to him and is strong willed enough to reject any other bids should they unexpectedly materialize. This attitude is more likely if the buyer shows willing from the start of the sale, by:

• Setting the finances and legal matters in motion immediately.

• Offering close enough to the asking price to leave other interested buyers little opportunity to beat his offer.

Acceptance
If the offer is accepted, it's time for a small celebration – you are a major step closer to buying your new home. But before breaking open that bottle of 'bubbly', there is a little 'housekeeping' to take care of…

• Confirm that the property is being taken off the market, if this has been agreed. The cynical among you might even ask friends to ring the agent after a few days and mention that they saw that property for sale, and ask if they can view it!

• Show willing by immediately providing your solicitor's details to the estate agent.

• Remain philosophical – a sale agreed is only half the battle.

Remember: An offer is given 'subject to contract'. This is an important phrase, and should be added to any offer you submit in writing. It is your 'get out' clause, and allows you to withdraw at any time up to exchange of contracts.

5

AFTER THE SALE IS AGREED

The Next Steps
Having agreed the sale, the next step is dependent upon the owner's situation. If he still needs to find a property to buy, it is sensible to wait before proceeding further. Avoid spending money until the chain is complete. If the chain is complete, or the owner is prepared to move out anyway, then fill in the mortgage forms and instruct your solicitor. The estate agent will send a 'Memorandum of Sale'. This letter confirms the sale and includes:

• The price agreed.
• Details of the purchaser, owner, and their solicitors.
• Conditions relating to the sale; for example, timescales.
• Items to remain at the property (fixtures and fittings).

Although this is not a legally binding document, it is important to check that the information is correct and includes the phrase 'subject to contract' (see opposite).

THE SOLICITOR
It is now time to put your solicitor to work and ask him to begin the legal process. You may be asked to pay for immediate

expenses, and to sign a copy of the solicitor's 'Business Terms and Conditions'. Proof of identity and address will also be required; for example, passport, driving licence, etc., to comply with money laundering regulations.

The solicitor will confirm that:

• You understand the commitment you are about to make.

• You have organized a mortgage lender and a deposit.

• You are aware of the finances needed to maintain a home.

The owner's solicitor will then send legal paperwork to your solicitor, although these procedures, including searches, are increasingly being done electronically. A buyer's solicitor will therefore expect the following:

• *A contract.* This document, called an 'Agreement Including Standard Conditions of Sale', contains both general matters relating to all sales, and those specific to yours. Two copies of the contract are sent to your solicitor for his approval. One will be retained, and the other sent back to the seller's solicitor once the details are approved (this will eventually be signed by the seller prior to the 'exchange of contracts').

• Copies of the *deeds* (title register) and if a leasehold property a copy of the lease.

• *Energy Performance Certificate (EPC).* This contains information about a property's energy use and typical energy costs, together with recommendations about how to reduce energy use and save money.

• *'Seller's Property Information Form'.* This is completed by the homeowner, and covers a wide range of subjects: the property's boundaries, guarantees for work undertaken at the property (double glazing, electrical work, etc.), disputes with neighbours, any alterations to the property and necessary permissions, and the proposed moving date. If a leasehold property is being sold, then an additional form, the 'Seller's Leasehold Information Form', will also be supplied, where appropriate. This confirms the length of lease, service and ground rent charges, and names those responsible for the upkeep of the building.

• *Fixtures and fittings list.*

Based on the answers in the Seller's Information Form, the buyer's solicitor may raise further questions, called 'additional enquiries'.

THE SEARCHES
Searches are documents dealing with the property that is being bought and the area surrounding it. There are several types of search, including:

• Local Authority Search. This is in two parts:

  1. The LLC1 form which details charges on the property such as conditional planning consents, improvement grants, tree preservation orders and conservation areas.

  2. The Con 29 form which covers matters under the council's jurisdiction; for example, proposed housing or commercial developments nearby, proposed new roads, etc.

• *Drainage Search.* Concerned with drainage and sewage in the area.

• *Environmental Search.* Depending on circumstances, this may be necessary if, for example, the property has been built on a landfill site or in an area of flooding. It covers a 500m radius of the building.

- *Coal Search*. This deals with information about any local mines; for example, for housing built in the neighbourhood of old mine shafts in areas such as Lancashire, Yorkshire, Derbyshire, Kent, or Warwickshire.

Mortgage and Survey

The relevant mortgage forms need to be completed and a survey fee paid. The latter is one of the most important stages of the buying process, and needs further explanation. Buying a first home is a major commitment. To be certain that a property is good security for the loan to be made against it, and fair value, you and/or the mortgage lender will employ a qualified surveyor to investigate matters pertaining to its construction, value and condition, and detail these in a report.

There are three types of surveys available:

- Mortgage lender's valuation.

- Home buyer's survey and valuation (also called homebuyer's report or homebuyer's service).

- Building survey (also known as a structural survey).

MORTGAGE LENDER'S VALUATION

This is the most basic of the three and mainly for the benefit of the lender. It confirms that the property is worthy of a mortgage. This is the least expensive type, sometimes free, and should not be relied upon to answer the questions necessary to make an informed decision about a purchase (its contents may not even be made available to the buyer).

HOME BUYER'S SURVEY AND VALUATION

Although more costly than the first, it is a far more detailed document. Written in a clear and understandable way, it is a standard form with the purpose of (a) offering an opinion on the sale price and (b) highlighting significant problems or defects that need immediate attention. If appropriate, any associated legal and environmental matters will also be mentioned. The 'home buyer's survey and valuation' is used for homes in average condition and of standard construction. Those buying a property which has been greatly altered, is in poor condition or of unusual construction, should consider our final survey type.

THE BUILDING SURVEY

This looks in depth at the property, and leaves 'few stones unturned'! Because it is concerned with condition, construction and defects both large and small, it is a lengthy document and consequently the most expensive. While the mortgage lender can arrange the first two types of survey, a buyer would need to commission this one himself.

Another question often asked by people purchasing a newly built home is whether a survey is really necessary. Apart from it being a prerequisite by the mortgage lender, it would be unwise to enter into a transaction without one, even for a very recently constructed home. While there should be a building guarantee called an 'NHBC Guarantee', it is better to be armed with as much information as possible before the purchase than regret it later should a problem appear. Only a survey can fulfil this.

Reading the Survey

Once completed, the survey is normally sent to the purchaser with the mortgage offer. For a first-time buyer, this might be his first experience of seeing a survey report. For those receiving the popular 'home buyer's survey and valuation', we have always thought it is very much like reading a national newspaper – you turn to the back page for the sports and then wade through the less important matters, like the economy and world politics!

The final page is one of the most interesting. It is the summary, and includes the surveyor's overall opinion of the property, its worth and any issues that need to be addressed.

As the complete report can be many pages long, it demands to be read slowly and several times. Use a marker to highlight passages or technical words not understood, and make notes in the margins as questions come to mind. The surveyor can then be called to answer these. If you have a good relationship with your solicitor, call on his expertise to offer a second opinion. The estate agent can be asked but remember that he represents the owner and may not have in-depth knowledge of building construction.

THE PROBLEM CLINIC

We have all heard terrible tales about problems which occur while buying a home. The majority of issues, however, are resolvable (otherwise, all estate agents would be poor!). While mentioning every problem that could occur would take a whole book of its own, here are some of the most common.

1. A POOR SURVEY

It is unlikely that the survey will be perfect. Properties are constructed with materials that, like everything else, are affected by normal wear and tear. The survey report may, therefore, unearth matters that need closer inspection.

- *Damp*. Moisture has penetrated the interior of a building. Unless extensive, it can be remedied for relatively little cost (although redecoration may be involved).

- *Woodworm*. Like damp, this is quite common and usually rectifiable, depending on how far it has spread.

- *Leaking roof*.

- *Leaking guttering*.

- *Electrical wiring*. Wiring that fails to conform to the most modern standards is not unusual. Ask the surveyor how much of an immediate or real problem this is.

Many purchasers, who are faced with any of these, panic and ask either for an immediate reduction on the price, or withdraw from the sale altogether. How can such decisions be made, though, without being in possession of all the facts? Instead, it is better to discover whether the problem is as severe as it seems, and how much it will cost to rectify. Bearing in mind the amount of time and effort already invested in the sale, what harm could there be in waiting a few more days for this information?

Arrange for specialists to visit the property and inspect the defects, i.e. a 'damp and woodworm' company, a roofer, etc. Organize two of each to call and offer an opinion and a price. (There may be costs involved, so check.)

Armed with their quotes, it is time to make a decision about the purchase. If the costs are small, you might decide to ignore the problem and continue with the sale. If not, then the seller is approached, via the estate agent, and a price reduction asked for, to take into account the extra money that now needs to be spent. To prove the request is legitimate, provide a copy of the survey and contractor's estimates. The estate agent will then report to the seller and return with one of three answers:

• The reduction is acceptable. The price is altered and the sale continues. (The solicitors and financial adviser need to be informed. A price reduction may affect the percentage of mortgage being obtained, which could have other 'knock on' effects. A financial adviser will be able to give guidance on this.)

• The owner refuses any reduction. The purchaser must now decide whether he wishes to continue at the original price (taking into account the money already spent, and the prospect of having to pay more for the next property if the market is rising).

- The owner wants to negotiate. Using the estate agent as an intermediary, you will try to find 'common ground' that keeps all parties happy.

We have lost track of the number of homes that are presented beautifully but ultimately return very poor survey reports.

The owners have spent a fortune on the superficial look of their home and totally ignored the fabric of the building.

This is like driving a Porsche but never having it serviced. It looks great but eventually those looks won't stop it from breaking down and costing thousands of pounds to fix.

Check everything before you buy – never rely just on what something looks like.

---

2. Undertaking Repairs

If the survey highlights necessary repairs, never ask the owner to undertake them. Instead, agree a reduction and arrange the work yourself. It is better to deal with tradesmen of your choosing and quality.

It is unlikely that the owner will allow this work to be undertaken immediately, preferring instead that you wait until after 'completion', when you have legal ownership of the property. The only exception might be when dealing with a property which is vacant and in need of renovation. The purchaser can then request access to the property after exchange and before completion to make the home habitable. The owner is under no obligation to agree, but consent is often considered if the purchaser signs a document called an 'undertaking', which outlines the jobs being carried out and confirms that the buyer will:

- Be liable for any damage caused.
- Agree not to take up residency until completion.

This can be organized through the solicitors, and is best agreed upon before exchange of contracts.

3. WITHDRAWING FROM A SALE

Occasionally, there may be the need to withdraw from a sale. This could be due to the buyer's situation altering suddenly, such as change of job or financial circumstances, or as the result of a poor survey. If so, inform your solicitor and the homeowner.

This may be unpleasant, but it is courteous. We have dealt with buyers who have decided against buying a property and failed to inform anyone for weeks! This is selfish and unnecessary.

4. THE OWNER'S SLOW SOLICITOR

If the owner's solicitor is proving slow in acting, then the buyer's solicitor needs to question why.

- Is the seller's solicitor simply over burdened with work?

- Has the seller's solicitor been told to slow the process down? Is the seller negotiating with another buyer? Does he have a hidden agenda that the buyer is unaware of? Is he having second thoughts about moving? Does the seller have a problem with the property he is hoping to buy? These questions can be asked by both the buyer's solicitor and by the estate agent. The latter will be keen to help as he is only paid when the sale is completed.

- Is the seller's solicitor in possession of all the necessary information? If not, when will these be ready?

5. MORTGAGE CONDITIONS

When the mortgage offer is issued, the purchaser needs to read it through carefully. Confirm that it contains the correct interest rate and amount to be borrowed. There will also be a section which outlines any conditions attached to the mortgage that need to be fulfilled. These might include further documents required by the mortgage lender, or additional reports on the building (such as an electrical inspection or damp report).

6. DEFECTIVE LEASE

One of the most important elements when buying a flat or maisonette is ensuring that the lease is satisfactory, as it defines the responsibilities and obligations of those who own properties in the building with regards to the freeholder and each owner of the flats.

As standards have changed over the years, your solicitor may feel that the lease is inadequate or has errors. Such defects might include insufficient details about assigning responsibilities for the foundation, roof and communal areas like hallways and landings. While this may come as a disappointment, it is a matter that can be rectified. A 'deed of variation' is required. As the name suggests, this is a legal term for a process which involves changing aspects of the lease to bring it in line with more modern procedures. It can take time to organize, and your solicitor will be able to advise as to whether it is worth pursuing.

7. LEASE EXTENSION

Another important aspect when buying a flat is the length of the lease. One in excess of 75–80 years is preferable. However, it may be possible to make an offer on a property with a shorter lease, but then extend it before the end of the transaction (completion). There will be costs involved:

• The cost of extending the lease.

• Solicitors' fees.

- Additional costs to other related parties, which includes paying the freeholder's costs; for example, to his managing agent who has supervision of the building on behalf of the freeholder, to his solicitor, and to his surveyor who 'values' the cost of extending the lease.

If the owner is keen to sell and the short lease is proving a problem, then he may bear the majority, if not all, of the costs and would be expected to extend the lease before completion. (The buyer should also be aware that one disadvantage of extending a lease is that it may mean the ground rent increases.)

8. INCORRECT DETAILS

If, as the sale progresses, it transpires that the property sheet given to the buyer by the estate agent was incorrect, action can be taken. Under the 1991 Property Misdescriptions Act (PMA) all property details supplied by an estate agent must be as accurate as possible. If not, then they may have breached the PMA. For example:

- The property details show that a flat has 97 years of lease but subsequent documentation shows it to be only 79 years.

- A garden described by the estate agent as 100 feet is actually 75 feet.

- A property that the estate agent suggests as being in good order actually requires modernization.

- A home marketed as 'new to the market' has been for sale for many months.

Such matters have gone unchecked in the past, but the PMA attempts to put paid to these 'errors'. If this situation arises, then:

- Approach the owner of the estate agency and explain the situation. He will want to rectify matters immediately and may offer to pay some compensation if inconvenience has been caused; for example, if a party has travelled some distance to view a property based on misleading information.

If this does not bring satisfactory results, then the next option is to:

- Call the local Trading Standards Office. They will investigate the matter and decide whether further action is needed. It is important to note that their assistance can be requested, even if you are not actually buying a property but simply in possession of property details that have been misleading. If necessary, they have the power to seize items from a company to prove a breach of the Property Misdescriptions Act. The act is enforced through the courts and, if found guilty, the company and individual involved can be subject to penalties such as a fine and even a criminal record.

9. BE PROACTIVE

Although we employ 'professionals' to deal with property sales, don't sit back and rely on them wholly. Keep in contact regularly and ask questions to confirm that everything is proceeding to plan. For example:

The Mortgage Broker

- Has the survey been organized. If not, why not?

- Have all the necessary employer's references and credit checks been sent to the mortgage lender?

- With the survey completed, when will the mortgage offer appear?

- If the mortgage offer is delayed, ask for specific reasons why.

The Solicitor
- Have the necessary documents been received from the owner's solicitor?

- If buying a flat, have all the documents relating to the lease and maintenance charges been received?

- If legal paperwork is outstanding, when is this to be chased and by whom?

The Estate Agent
- The agent has the best overall view of the sale and any associated chain. He is ideally placed to chase:

- Outstanding paperwork.
- Delayed surveys.
- And to keep abreast of progress in the chain.

Never be afraid to ring and ask your estate agent for advice; it is in his financial interest for the sale to be successful. There is little an estate agent cannot do if he is experienced and skilful.

Preparing for Exchange
With any problems resolved, the next step is exchange of contracts. This is the point of no return, at which the owner becomes legally bound to sell, and the purchaser legally bound to buy.

THE SOLICITOR
Before exchange of contracts, the solicitor will need to be in possession of all of the necessary legal information, comprising:

- Contract.
- Searches.
- Enquiries.
- Satisfactory mortgage offer.
- Leasehold documents if a flat is being bought.
- Transfer documents.
- Deposit.

The purchaser will then visit the solicitor's office (or use the post/email/fax, etc.) to discuss these matters and take any final advice. Confirm that the sale includes all that was expected, in particular that:

- The 'fixtures and fittings' list is in order.

- The completion date is correct (when deciding on this, take into account the availability of removal vans).

- If it was requested that areas be cleared of all rubbish (i.e. garage or loft) has this been included in the contract?

- Are all the keys to be made available on completion? Few things could be more annoying than to find that keys to the garage or kitchen window have gone missing.

The contract is then signed.

DEPOSIT AND ADDITIONAL COSTS
The solicitor will require a deposit. This is normally 5 to 10 per cent of the purchase price, and non-returnable after exchange. A banker's draft, electronic transfer or building society cheque is preferable. If notice needs to be given to obtain the deposit, then the purchaser should organize this in plenty of time. Because of growing fears about money laundering (money obtained from the proceeds of crime and transformed into legitimate funds), cash will not be acceptable.

The buyer will also need to arrange buildings insurance so that it can be initiated immediately after exchange. Lastly, and we only mention it again because of the large sums involved, remember that 'stamp duty' is payable by the purchaser. (The solicitor usually requests payment of stamp duty after exchange and prior to completion.)

THE 'EXCHANGE'

With everything organized, and the chain ready, 'exchange of contracts' can take place. This is carried out over the telephone between the solicitors in the chain. The purchaser need not be present.

It is far from an exciting event and consists of the purchaser's solicitor saying, for example, to the owner's solicitor:

'I release the contract to you under Law Society Formula B.'[1]

The contract is now released, which means that the purchaser's solicitor promises that for a fixed period of time he will not withdraw from the transaction. With this guarantee, the seller's solicitor can now follow the same process on the property his client is buying. This conversation therefore is duplicated by each solicitor up the chain until it reaches the top, and all contracts are released. Calls to confirm the exchange happen next, to each link back down the chain.

With exchange of contracts, the finishing line is in sight; the day when you take ownership of your new home, known as Completion.

Because the period leading up to this involves so many elements common to both buyer and seller, this final part of our journey is dealt with jointly, in Part Three, starting on page 137.

---

1. There are in fact three legal mechanisms for exchanging contracts, formulas A, B and C.

PART TWO

THE SELLER

6

PREPARATION

Part Two of the book is mainly aimed at those who are selling property, and wish to understand how the property market works today. In addition, this part will also be extremely useful to the buyer. The advice given here will enable a buyer to appreciate the seller's point of view; by seeing the whole procedure from the opposite perspective, a much better and more balanced picture emerges.

The purchase and sale of property is one of the very few areas of British life that involves financial negotiation, so it is an experience that is largely foreign to most of us, and that is why it is so useful to understand both sides.

Introduction

Many years ago, while studying for his degree, Paul attended a classical music concert. He didn't particularly want to go, but felt obliged, as many of the performers in the orchestra were friends. It didn't help that he knew they were poorly prepared for the concert.

The highlight of the evening was the performance of a beautiful symphony by Cesar Franck. As the conductor raised his baton and the orchestra started to play, one of my course tutors, who was sitting in the audience, remarked rather loudly,

'What's the point in playing the rest of the piece if they can't even get the first note in tune?'

Paul has never forgotten this. It serves as a good reminder that thorough preparation is vital before we begin any task. Those who have read the buyer section of this book will already be acquainted with this idea, and it is just as true for the seller. Careful planning will save time in the end, and help avoid many of the pitfalls to which others have fallen prey.

Preparation is VITAL!

This chapter is divided into four sections:

- Preparing our home.
- Preparing the paperwork.
- Preparing our finances.
- Preparing ourselves.

Preparing Our Home

Preparing a property for sale has become a popular subject in the media. This is hardly surprising. It is as crucial to finding a buyer as are location and accommodation. We learnt early in our careers that the longer an applicant spends at a property, the more likely he is to buy it. This is a good principle to remember.

If the environment is welcoming, then people are likely to stay longer and feel a greater bond with the property. This is achieved by appealing to three of our five senses: sight, sound, and smell. With these we form opinions about the world around us. Unfortunately, this can be an immediate, and sometimes unfair, reaction. If a prospective buyer walks up the path to your home and is greeted with a shabby front door, he'll have a poor opinion of the property before he even sets foot in the hallway. The fact that you may have a splendid modern kitchen or beautiful marble tiled bathroom is immaterial; his mind is made up and will be difficult to change. Subconsciously he starts wondering what other problems may be lurking that are not so obvious.

This issue can be a particular challenge when selling a flat, where you are reliant on others keeping the communal parts of the block looking spotless. When Paul sold his flat many years ago, he took ten minutes before a viewing to pick up any litter in the communal areas and spray air freshener around the entrance.

A PERFECT WORLD
Why are first impressions so important? Because the public often cannot be bothered to see beyond the blemishes. If a place is scruffy and there are five other homes to see that day, why waste time with this one? To do our home justice, we need to be honest and objective.

- Could the paintwork in the lounge do with a little freshening up?

- Would the bathroom be better without the patches of condensation on the ceiling?

- And, for those of you who are keen on DIY, don't you think it's time to complete those wardrobes in the bedroom that you started building last summer?

It is difficult to be self critical because all of us become accustomed to our homes. We have met many homeowners who didn't appreciate that leaving piles of food crumbs all over the kitchen, or the dog's food partly in its bowl, but mostly on the kitchen floor, is a 'turn off' to buyers. Untidiness is another aspect. Imagine walking into a room littered with books and children's toys. How can a buyer appreciate its size or potential?

If we do not remedy these matters, then we are doing our home a disservice. As sellers, we must consider how others will view it. If keeping a family house constantly tidy is a strain, then perhaps:

- Limit the children/pets to one room, just prior to a viewing.

- Arrange appointments for specific times, during which the property can be kept in an orderly fashion.

However you remedy the situation it will pay dividends. The more the public like our home, the more they are likely to pay for it.

FURTHER IMPROVEMENTS
Cosmetic improvements are only one area that can visually enhance a property. Light, for example, plays an important role; opening curtains during the day gives the impression of an airy room. Alternatively, if it's dark or cloudy outside, switch the lights on (if it's cold as well, then turn the thermostat up).

To appeal to our sense of sound, keep windows shut if you live on a busy main road, or play soothing classical music. This is infinitely more inviting than leaving the television on.

As regards smell, pleasing fragrances are a great help in producing a positive experience for our viewer. Baking bread has always been a popular example, and there are many super-market fragrances that mask the everyday smells of cigarettes and cooking. Included in this category are pets. It is easy to become accustomed to their odour and be oblivious to it per-meating carpets and furnishings. If anything is guaranteed to cause a potential purchaser to flee, with no intention of ever returning, it is the overpowering smell of animals. The remedy is simple: clean the garden before an appointment and mask the smell of pets. Remember that some people are allergic to or frightened of pets, so it might even be preferable to keep animals shut away during a viewing.

These improvements cost little. Avoid major expenditure. Spend your money on your new home rather than on your present one. The only exception would be obvious defects that may be highlighted in a buyer's survey, such as broken guttering or a leaking roof. As a rule of thumb, if a problem can be resolved for a few hundred pounds then consider sorting it. Otherwise, expect to be asked for a discount at the offer stage or after a survey.

Preparing the Paperwork
Organizing the paperwork is often overlooked, and is particularly important for properties which have undergone structural alteration. Some of the most depressing times we had as estate agents involved selling houses with incomplete documentation. We'd find a buyer for them, and all would go well until it transpired that the owners didn't have all the legal documents needed for the extended kitchen, or the bedroom in the loft. Either the sale then fell apart, or it became a long drawn out affair as the owners tried to obtain the relevant documents. With a little forward planning this could have been organized before marketing.

Keeping receipts for major jobs such as reproofing or rewiring is also vital. Anyone can claim to have had new plumbing installed two years ago. Reinforce this with paperwork and yours will be 'head and shoulders' above the average home for sale. Flat owners will need a copy of their lease, and receipts confirming the payment of the service charge or ground rent. These are obtained from the party who receives these monies, i.e. the freeholder, managing agent or residents' association. Many an undecided purchaser has been persuaded to buy a particular property because of such diligence.

Until recently, title deeds were also required as proof of ownership. While for many this is still a valid system, title deeds are now redundant for property transactions completed after 13 October 2003. They instead have a document issued by the Land Registry called a Title Information Document.

Plainly both systems will be in use for a number of years and, if in doubt about the whereabouts of any of these items, consult your solicitor. In fact, this is the ideal time for those without a solicitor to shop around and make a choice. He can help prepare the paperwork in anticipation of securing a buyer. This is a subject that was covered in more detail on page 58.

Preparing Our Finances
Two questions regarding our finances need to be asked:

• If we intend to buy another property when ours is sold, can we obtain the necessary loan?

• Will redeeming the present mortgage incur any penalties with our mortgage lender?

We dealt with a young couple who found a buyer for their home, only to discover later that redeeming their mortgage early would incur a huge penalty. This was so unexpected it almost derailed the sale. Fortunately, the situation was rectified but not before many sleepless nights were had by all.

Preparing Ourselves
With the paperwork, finances and property organized, just one more item remains... preparing ourselves.

Never let selling your home rule your life.

We have met too many people, particularly first-time sellers, who allow their sale to dominate them completely. Every waking hour is spent thinking about it. Quickly, all sense of perspective is lost; a small problem, that could be easily resolved, becomes overwhelming. It is impossible to see 'light at the end of the tunnel', and everything becomes an effort. Stress is setting in.

Selling a property is only a very small part of our lives, and should be treated as such. It is important, but not to the detriment of our well being. For example, if you eat at 7 pm then leave this hour free, rather than rushing the meal because you have a 7.30 viewing. If children are in bed by 8 pm, then finish viewings by 7.45. The public will understand.

However, you may need to be flexible if a viewer is coming a long distance to see your property and only has limited time available. You don't want to lose a possible sale because you refused to alter your usual routine!

7

CHOOSING AN ESTATE AGENT

Mr and Mrs Average want to buy a car. They visit the showroom and immediately see a vehicle they like. The salesman approaches and starts his sales pitch, explaining how wonderful the car is, its sleek lines, ample boot, fast acceleration and spacious interior. Our couple has certain requirements but instead of asking any questions, they base their decision solely on the salesman's information.

Only once the car is delivered do they realize it is a little smaller than they had wanted, the fuel consumption is not as economical as first thought, and the warranty is only for one year not the two they had expected. Quickly they regret their decision.

Obviously, this situation is ridiculous. Who would buy a car on this basis? It is instead a painstaking process, involving preparation, research, and comparison of a number of vehicles. So, when selling our most expensive asset, our home, why does this common sense approach disappear? Many homeowners give as little thought to choosing an estate agent as Mr and Mrs Average did to choosing a car. No wonder, then, that so many regret their choice. However, a remedy is at hand.

Whom to Call?

In some ways, estate agents are very similar to cars; different firms offer different features. Although superficially they may look similar, once you peek under the bonnet and ask more probing questions, differences emerge. Your method, therefore, is to ask several estate agents to visit your home (called a valuation or market appraisal), question them thoroughly and, based on this meeting, decide who best fulfils your needs.

It is worth mentioning that it is now perfectly possible to deal with agents who simply 'exist' on the internet. These are companies who have no shop front and who you might never 'meet in the flesh'. While some might visit and provide a conventional 'valuation' service, and perhaps even handle the entire sales process for you (as a standard estate agent might), others will instead rely on you supplying your own details and asking price. They all have one thing in common though; marketing is undertaken on the 'net'. If you follow this route, then it is vital to confirm at the start exactly what level of service is provided. It might be cheaper than a high street estate agent but is this false economy going to be a hindrance later when a problem arises, you need help and there is no one to turn to?

The remainder of the book has presumed that a seller wishes to follow the conventional estate agent route, as for the inexperienced seller this seems the safest route to take. This may, of course, change in the future, depending on how the internet develops.

Our First Step

Your first step is to create a shortlist of companies, by researching the following:

DOMINANCE IN THE AREA

Drive around your area, and it will quickly become clear, from the 'For Sale' and 'Sold' boards, which companies are most popular in your neighbourhood.

WORD OF MOUTH
Neighbours who have already dealt with agents can be useful in helping to decide who is worthy of your attention.

HIGH STREET POSITION
Which companies have a prime position on the high street? This should guarantee them plenty of passing trade to take an interest in your home, and so increase the number of prospective buyers.

OPENING HOURS
Which agents open early or close late? A 9 to 5.30 approach could miss commuters passing by the office on their way to and from work.

ADVERTISING
This is the section of the book that has probably changed the most since the first and second editions. Who could have predicted even five years ago how much the web and social media would change our lives? This is certainly true for the property agent. They now have at their disposal, not only the traditional printed advertising (i.e. newspapers and magazines) but also such digital marketing as twitter, facebook, web portals, smart phone apps etc, etc.

In no particular order we would suggest as far as advertising is concerned that you check out an agent in the following areas:

1. Which agents provide websites that look professional, and are easy to navigate? There are few agents that don't have sites so check on their appearance. This is often a good indication as to the worth of an agent. A site that looks as if it cost less than a pint of beer to produce could suggest that this is likely to be an agent running things on a shoestring. If they have little to spend on advertising, then perhaps they

have a similar issue when employing quality staff to help you successfully sell your home.

2. Which agents use social media to market and sell property? A local agent to us regularly tweets to his followers immediately he markets a new instruction. Social media in general, unlike newspapers and emails, do offer the opportunity to communicate with potential buyers in a very quick and effective way.

3. In addition to an agency's own website, many agents rely on marketing property through a web portal. This includes such sites as Right Move and Zoopla who collect property information from many hundreds of agents and make them all available on their website. This makes it far easier for a buyer, who may not know the names of individual agents in an area, to visit a property web portal and simply search for properties for sale by location.

4. Even with the advent of digital media, there are still agents who find an audience of potential buyers in newspapers and magazines. It would be worth discussing this with the agent of your choice, for their opinion on its worth in your area.

5. We have no doubt that five minutes after this book is published a new method of marketing property through the web or social media will appear! A word of caution. Not every new innovation will be effective for selling your property, so should an agent offer you a new gimic – beware! Always ask them to provide evidence on its effectiveness. Do not become a guinea-pig!

A few years ago Paul was looking to buy a home near where he worked, and was shocked by how many agents, when he called for property details, simply dismissed the request for help by telling him to visit their website.

Where was the customer service or selling skills that presumably their sellers are paying for?

TYPES OF ESTATE AGENTS

There are two types of estate agents:

- Those owned by a large organization, a bank or building society for example, with offices around the country.

- Those that are independent, probably run by the owners, and boasting a more personal service.

QUALIFICATIONS

No longer is simply being a good salesman sufficient. The public now want only to deal with estate agents who can prove their level of expertise. This is now possible with nationally recognized qualifications called the Technical Award qualification and the Certificate Qualification, both available from the National Federation of Property Professionals. These prove that an agent has at least a minimum level of knowledge with which to help the seller secure a sale that successfully completes.

For peace of mind, confirm that the agent you choose has one of these qualifications. You could also call them or use their website to request property details, to discover their level of service.

With all the answers to the above, narrow the list of possible agents to three and invite them round.

What is Required from an Estate Agent?

This might seem a strange question, as obviously an estate agent is required to:

- Provide a market appraisal (suggest an asking price for your home).

- Market the property.

- Find a buyer at a satisfactory figure.

This, however, is only half the story. His true role is to use his knowledge and experience to:

- Identify the *best* possible buyer for your home.

- Negotiate an acceptable figure.

- Manage the sale, and have the depth of knowledge and experience to resolve any problems that occur along the way (so reducing your stress level as much as possible).

These last three are services that estate agents should provide, and which members of the public cannot reasonably accomplish themselves, because they lack experience.

The Valuation
Before a property can be marketed, an agent will visit and offer an opinion on price. Ask three to come, and arrange for all three agents to call on the same day, to make the comparisons easier. Each agent will want to inspect the property, and take written details to refer to later in the meeting. Use the opportunity to follow the agent around and engage him in conversation. Find out:

- How long he has been in the profession.
- Whether he has a recognized qualification (see above).
- How well he knows the area.

You are beginning to accumulate information to help decide how competent he is, and whether you feel comfortable with him.

The Presentation

The most important part of the meeting has been reached: the presentation. This is your visitor's opportunity to set out his wares and persuade you to instruct him. Prepare yourself for a 15 to 20 minute 'performance', but remember that the agent's purpose is to persuade you to use his services by providing positive information about his company. Your job is to prise details from him that are not so forthcoming! This is achieved by asking a series of prepared questions.

1. MARKETING

What newspapers would be used to promote your home, and how frequently?
Local newspapers are a common form of media advertising. There are two types: the 'free' paper that is delivered to homes, and the 'bought' paper which is available from newsagents. The latter have the advantage of being available to those moving from outside the area. Often a company will use both, to reach as wide an audience as possible.

Those with colour advertisements may be more striking than black and white ones, as well as those that use larger, more noticeable photographs.

Is newspaper advertising included in the commission fee?
It is usual practice for estate agents to advertise weekly in the local newspapers and include this in their fee.

However, if this is not the case and there are extra charges involved for newspaper advertising, the agent needs to declare this in his written business terms and conditions. Although unlikely for a first-time seller's home, should you wish to have your property marketed somewhere not normally dealt with by the agent (for example, in a glossy magazine), this too should be agreed prior to signing a contract.

2. INTERNET AND TECHNOLOGY
What does an agency's website look like?
In recent years, technology has gradually changed the way estate agents work. In particular, most agents rely on a website for their marketing. This provides round-the-clock advertising. (See pages 85–86 for additional information.)

However, it is important for you to establish what other methods of marketing the agent uses. For example, will prospective buyers be alerted to the sale of your home through text messaging or email alerts?

3. PROPERTY DETAIL SHEETS
What are they like?
Even though websites are important for selling property, there are members of the public who still expect to be given a printed detail sheet on your property.

Therefore, it is important that they send the right signals to a prospective buyer. Ask to see a sample. Inexpensive digital cameras, desktop publishing and laser printing allow a professional looking detail sheet to be created easily. Internal shots enhance the look and quality, and are a contributing factor to persuading a potential buyer to visit your property.

4. 'FOR SALE' BOARDS
Will one be used?
Erecting a 'For Sale' board is highly desirable.

• It helps to locate the property; useful for night time viewings and properties on a main road.

• If neighbours have a friend or relative wanting to move into the area, a board alerts them that there is an impending sale.

A property must be exposed to as wide an audience as possible, and few things are better than a board.

They are most effective at the start of the marketing process, where the aim is to alert the world that your property is for sale. It would be a pity to miss such an opportunity, especially as the board is probably included as part of the agent's fee, and surely one of a homeowner's goals is to 'get his money's worth' out of the agent!

Are you allowed to erect a board? This question is directed mainly towards owners of flats who might:

• Share their front garden and need permission from other parties in the building.

• Be restricted by the terms and conditions in the lease from having a board.

Always check.

5. RECENT SIMILAR SALES
What properties has the agent sold recently in your area which are similar to your own?
The answer should confirm that:

• The agent does indeed sell homes in your vicinity.

• He sells your type of property. An agent that specializes in detached houses may struggle to sell a flat. He may have few of the right type of buyers on his books; he may also be inexperienced in marketing that sort of home.

6. WHO WILL DEAL WITH THE SALE?
If someone senior is conducting the market appraisal, will he also be dealing with your sale?
If not, and you are placed in the hands of a junior member of staff:

- Will he be visiting, to have first-hand information when describing your property to interested clients?

- How experienced is he? Will he have the skills needed to assist you throughout the sale? As we have already mentioned, the quality of the staff has a significant bearing on the sale of your home, and the smooth progress of the transaction.

7. OPENING HOURS
What are the opening hours?
Estate agents normally work longer hours than most other high street businesses. 9 am to 6 pm is common for weekdays, 9 am to 4 pm on a Saturday, and some open on a Sunday. Don't let any agent suggest that a website is a substitute for not opening long hours.

8. NUMBER OF HOMES FOR SALE
How many properties does the agent have for sale at any time?
Are you one of many hundreds vying for their attention and advertising space, or do they value quality over quantity and offer all clients the personal attention they deserve?

Avoid becoming just another entry on their computer database. Selling a home is a very personal experience and you want the agent to give you individual attention.

9. MARKETING STRATEGY
How does the agent intend to use marketing to secure you a buyer?

- At what point will he review marketing progress with you?

- What happens if your home remains unsold? How will the situation be resolved?

You are embarking on a journey that only the foolhardy would attempt without a map to guide them. Asking the agent for a marketing strategy is a good test of his experience. If he tackles the question before you ask it, this is a good sign. If he flounders and is unprepared, is he really the agent for you?

10. ONGOING COMMITMENT
What services are provided once an offer has been made?
It is after an offer has been made that the estate agent's job takes on a new significance, by:

• Knowing the appropriate questions to ask a buyer to assess the suitability of the offer.

• Investigating his answers.

• Negotiating a sale.

• Managing the sale until its conclusion, using skill and expertise to resolve any problems along the way.

This is an agent's true role, and any that fail to realize this should be avoided.

11. COMMISSION
What is the fee?
'Pay peanuts, get monkeys' is apt here. Choose an agent who charges a minimal amount, for example 0.5 per cent, and don't be surprised to find that the services he provides are not as good as you may have hoped. He is unlikely to have the funds to afford decent advertising, or quality staff. Your goal is to find an agent who will sell your home at a satisfactory price and in an acceptable timescale. This demands one with skill, and an organization with a high level of service. These are features worth paying for.

In an effort to keep costs down, it is human nature for the seller to use the commission level as a deciding factor. This is short sighted. A 'cheap and cheerful' agent is not necessarily the best approach. Often a company's fees are low because this is the only way they can secure business. As a general guide, commission rates range from 1 per cent plus VAT to 2 per cent plus VAT for sole agency instructions, and 1.5 per cent to 2.5 per cent for multiple agency instructions. A good average to pay would be 1.5 per cent plus VAT for a sole agency instruction and 2–2.5 per cent for a multiple agency instruction.

It is also important for a homeowner to be aware of fees before instructing an agent, and under the Estate Agents Act it is the latter's responsibility to give his charges to a homeowner (in writing and prior to being instructed). Charges should be clear and any additional costs should be mentioned. These might include:

• Media advertising (as discussed earlier).

• A 'For Sale' board. (There is unlikely to be any charge for this as it is such a good advertising opportunity for the agent.)

• VAT. This is likely to be on top of the main percentage fee. Finally, discussing fees with an agent is a good opportunity to test his negotiating skills, which you will be relying on later to obtain the highest price for your home. Imagine the point in the market appraisal where the agent has just explained his fee. Because other companies are also being considered, you ask if that is the best he can do. Would he consider reducing the fee for you? The agent who immediately obliges without any argument should be avoided; he lacks competent negotiating skills. However, find one who attempts to persuade you that his level of service, knowledge and expertise warrant the fee being asked, and this bodes well for the future. He may subsequently offer a slight discount as an incentive but this is good business practice rather than commercial weakness.

12. ACCOMPANIED VIEWINGS
Will the agent accompany those viewing your home?
Many homeowners are uncomfortable about showing strangers around their property. Apart from the matter of security, they worry about being drawn into conversations they are unprepared for, about such things as offers.

Confirm that the agent will attend every appointment. If you supply him with a front door key, ask about his arrangements for storing this safely.

13. TYPE OF AGENCY
What are the options?
There are three common ways to employ the services of an estate agent:

1. *Sole Agency.* A single company is used to market the property. This is a popular option. The agent should show you a high degree of loyalty because you have entrusted him to be your only representative. This strengthens the relationship and ensures a better level of service.

2. *Multiple Agency.* More than one company is asked to market your home. The fee, which is normally greater than that for sole agency, is given to the company which sells the property.

It is often presumed that this situation increases the possibility of finding a buyer. Sometimes the opposite is true. A property being marketed by several agencies may suggest to the public that either:

• The owner is desperate to sell.

Or:

• A single agent is unable to sell the property because there is something wrong with it.

Sending out such signals may cause prospective purchasers to view your home with caution, or put forward lower offers.

3. *Joint Sole Agency.* Two separate agencies are employed to market the property, and work together. The agreed fee is divided between them in an agreed proportion, regardless of who eventually sells the property. Using two agencies in differing localities widens the area of marketing, but without the disadvantages of using 'multiple agency'.

These matters should be outlined in the estate agent's contract, which he will probably ask you to sign. It defines the relationship between you both, and the obligations of each party. As with all contracts, careful reading is essential. Resist the temptation to sign it immediately. It should include:

- Commission payable (plus VAT).

- When the fee is payable.

- Any additional charges; for example, for photographs, 'For Sale' board, advertising, etc.

- *Contract Period.* The length of the contract and the restrictions it imposes should be made clear. The period agreed needs to be long enough for the agent to market your home properly, but short enough for you to be able to end it if the agent is not performing satisfactorily. Four to eight weeks is reasonable. Notice may need to be given if the contract is to be terminated.

- *Asking Price.* Check that the asking price quoted is the agreed figure.

- *Services* may be offered to potential buyers such as mortgage or removal services. The agent must make any services clear to the homeowner in writing prior to the buyer accepting them, as the agent potentially stands to gain financially from the acceptance of any services.

14. THE ASKING PRICE

This is one of the most important points. For most homeowners, the highlight of the market appraisal is discussing the asking price. There are two rules, however, that a homeowner breaks at his peril. Before the agent recommends an asking price, never:

- Suggest a figure yourself.

- Answer the estate agent's question, 'So Mr Homeowner, what figure did you want for your property?'

If the agent is incapable of offering a figure without guidance from you, then he does not deserve your business.

Ask for two figures: a realistic one, and something more optimistic that can be attempted for a short period. The first is used for budgeting for the next purchase, while the second allows the property to be 'tested' on the market for a few weeks. This is long enough to gauge the public's reaction and for the owner to prove that he had attempted as high an asking price as possible. The price can then be reduced if the property doesn't sell. The danger of asking a realistic figure immediately is that you find yourself with three offers within a few days, and wonder whether you could have achieved more.

'It is easier to come down in price than it is to go up' is a good rule to remember.

This route is only possible if the homeowner is in no great hurry and the market is active. In a poorly performing market, or where a quick sale is required, asking a reasonable figure immediately is more sensible.

A Little Creativity

For properties that are a little unusual or feature a standard of decoration and fitments above average, the seller can try different ways to price and market them:

- *The 'Guidance Only' technique.* Precede the asking price with the phrase 'Offers in the region of . . .'. For example, imagine a flat that has been the subject of complete renovation, to an extremely high standard. It is priced at 'Offers in the region of £200,000'. Applicants with a desire to purchase something different and above average may generate great demand. The phrase 'Offers in the region of . . .' has only suggested a price range. It does not limit the offers to £200,000 or lower, but allows for offers higher than £200,000. These may appear if there is healthy competition for the property.

- *Open House.* This is ideal for properties that command a great deal of interest, such as the luxury flat in our previous example. Instead of allowing people to visit your home at their convenience, limit the viewings to a two-hour window on just one or two days each week. Interested parties will now have to see your home at the same time, so increasing the sense of competition. Working on the assumption that buyers always want what they can see others are interested in, this should help to secure a sale at a good figure. This method of marketing can be combined with the 'sealed bid' technique of inviting offers. Use the 'guidance only' pricing discussed above and then request that all offers be sent to the agent's office in a sealed envelope by a certain date. This too increases the sense of competition and may result in a buyer offering more than anticipated in order to beat the others. Finally it should be mentioned that one of the disadvantages of an open house is security. Due to numerous strangers visiting the property at the same time, all valuables and items of sentimental value should be removed.

Word of Warning

Whatever techniques are used to market and price your property, you still need the agent's guidance on what amount is ultimately achievable. Be wary of an agent who only suggests one figure that seems hugely inflated. This could be an effort to impress, and obtain the instruction. While an optimistic price is flattering to the ego, an unrealistic one will leave the property unsold and the owner frustrated. Check the validity of the agent's recommendation by asking for comparable evidence of similar homes achieving such a price.

Valuing property is not an exact science and, ultimately, it's the public who determine the final selling figure. An asking price on a home is simply that – a price being asked, not necessarily its value. Finding the ideal asking price is a balancing act; it needs to be:

• Realistic enough to prevent the property remaining on the market for months.

But:

• High enough to ensure that the seller achieves the best price possible.

Several factors affect the price achieved. These include:

Location

I'm sure you have heard the old joke, what three things do you need to sell a property? 'Location, Location, Location.' Not particularly funny, but definitely true.

For example, if your home backs onto a railway line or is on a busy main road, then it's advisable to make an allowance for this in the price. The amount of 'allowance' will differ from area to area, and will depend on how people view the particular disadvantage. An experienced agent will be able to guide you on this.

In recent years, telecommunication masts and electricity pylons have also become factors that can affect the price of property (often dramatically) because, rightly or wrongly, health issues have been linked to these features.

THERE IS A BUYER FOR EVERYTHING!
'At the right price every property has a suitable buyer' is our philosophy and here is an example.

A few years ago we were instructed to sell a detached bungalow in North Harrow, Middlesex. It was an attractive looking property, with fair sized rooms and was not badly situated for the local shops and Metropolitan Line station. However standing at the end of the small back garden was an enormous electricity pylon. It dwarfed the bungalow, despite some effort having been made to plant trees to screen it, and it was so close that one could hear the 'buzz' of the power constantly. It was priced competitively, but needless to say it sat on the market. That was until an elderly lady came into our office looking for a ground floor flat/maisonette. She viewed the bungalow and was delighted as she thought she would never find a freehold property in her price range. She was hard of hearing so said the 'buzzing noise' would not trouble her. Any associated health risks being discussed at the time did not bother her either, due to her age. Thus the perfect buyer was found, and both parties were happy!

Condition

The second factor affecting price is 'condition', as previously discussed on page 77.

Timescales

If you are very keen to sell as soon as possible, then ask a realistic figure to secure a quick sale but accept it only on the basis that the buyer is able to proceed immediately, within the seller's timescales, and that no further reductions in price will be considered.

Stamp Duty Land Tax

One other factor might affect the price of a property: stamp duty. The current rates and thresholds are explained on page 22; at or near the thresholds this issue now affects the amount that people are willing to offer on a property. For example, a home bought for £249,000 will have stamp duty of £2,490 (1% x £249,000) payable. However, buying a property for £255,000 greatly increases the amount of stamp duty because it is now in the 3 per cent stamp duty bracket; £7,650 (3% x £255,000), over £5,000 difference!

This can result in an applicant making a lower offer on your home to bring it into a cheaper stamp duty bracket. A seller whose property price sits just above one of the stamp duty thresholds has two options to counter this 'problem':

• Concede that this is an injustice but you can't buck the system. Ask a price just below the stamp duty threshold, and widen its appeal to those conscious of the extra costs involved in buying a home in the higher stamp duty bracket.

• Disregard the stamp duty factor but appreciate that a buyer might make an offer to bring it into a lower bracket.

In the past there was a small loophole, which offered the homeowner a further option. Because no stamp duty is payable on fixtures and fittings, a property could be bought for an amount that brought it into a lower stamp duty bracket. Extra money would then be given to the seller for fixtures and fittings. However, such manipulation of the system has been recognized by HM Revenue & Customs, who now demand that a form (Land Transaction Return) be completed by the buyer detailing this matter. Questions will be asked if the amounts attributed to fixtures and fittings are unreasonable. Both you and the buyer need to check with your solicitors that the amount allocated is acceptable and justified.

8

THE APPOINTMENT

With all the preparations complete, you are now ready to throw open your doors to the public. Because this involves having strangers in your home, sensible precautions need to be taken. It is best for the estate agent to accompany prospective buyers around your home, although this is not always possible especially after working hours. In these circumstances, the homeowner's security is of paramount importance:

- All appointments must be arranged via the estate agent, with any 'unexpected viewers' being politely directed to the agent and not given access. Keep a supply of your agent's business cards by the door to hand to these people.

- Keep a note of all the arranged viewings. Record names, times, and numbers attending. During a single appointment (as opposed to an 'open house'), restrict the number of people visiting to a manageable two or three at one time. If there are more in the family, the others can call another time if necessary.

- Never be alone when showing someone around your home. Ensure a friend or family member is with you.

- Keep viewers in sight at all times, never turn your back and always keep a path clear to an exit.

- Ensure that valuables and items of sentimental value are hidden.

- Avoid appointments after 8.30 pm; there is no need to have strangers in your home any later.

Apart from security issues, here are a few tips to help enhance the viewing:

- Choose times when your home looks its best; Monday mornings, after a weekend of partying or energetic children, may not be ideal.

- Confirm with the estate agent that the viewers have full details of your home before they call. How frustrating would it be to discover after a 15 minute appointment that your visitors thought your flat was three bedroom rather than two, or £90,000 when you are actually asking £150,000!

- For evening viewings have an outside light on to help locate the property and, if possible, leave a handy parking space available for your visitor.

The Viewing
One of the questions most commonly asked by homeowners is:

'What do I do or say during the viewing?'

The answer is: very little. If the preparation stage has been completed thoroughly, then there is no need for any slick sales patter. Instead, our aim is simply to make this a positive and enjoyable experience; one that the viewer will remember long after the event.

First impressions have the greatest influence on potential buyers. Generally, people tend to remember the beginning and end of the visit more than the middle. Use this to your advantage by guiding them towards the very best features at the start and end of the 'tour'. Leading them immediately from the front door into your flat's lounge with its panoramic views, for example, is a wonderful way to start; strolling around the communal gardens could be a memorable end. What a lasting impression this will leave! Infinitely more powerful than attempting any high powered sales technique.

This isn't to suggest we can't give matters a helping hand; a few well chosen words is all it takes. Never overwhelm the viewer with too much information, just occasionally provide details that illustrate how happy you've been in your home and how much care you've lavished on it. The visitor's bond with your home will grow, and strengthen his desire to buy. This sense of connection can be further enhanced at the end of the visit, by asking if the viewer has any questions or would like to wander round once more. We were taught very early in our careers that the longer a person stays in your home, imagining living there, the greater connection he feels with it.

QUESTIONS
Be ready for the most common questions asked by viewers:

- What are your reasons for moving?
- Have you found a property to buy?
- How quickly do you want to move?
- What are the neighbourhood or local schools like?
- How far is it to the station?

We want to focus briefly on the first of these. Over the years we have dealt with people who have struggled to sell their home because of the way they answered this question.

'What are your reasons for moving?'
'Well we're not sure if we're moving yet.'

Or:

'What are your reasons for moving?'
'We're just testing the market to see what figure we can achieve for our home.'

Why would anyone want to consider a business transaction with someone so undecided? This is so much better:

'What are your reasons for moving?'
'As soon as we secure a buyer on our home we'll be looking to buy one nearer to my parents.'

This suggests commitment and a definite intention to move, from the type of serious minded people that can be trusted and relied on.

We are not suggesting we mislead anyone, but if a seller has a genuine desire to sell, then it's better to describe the situation in a more positive way.

The Close
There is a tendency at the end of a viewing, when everyone is unsure what to say, for a buyer to utter the immortal phrase:

'I'm definitely interested and I'll ring the agent with an offer.'

To all sellers, learn from the experiences of other homeowners; until this actually happens, don't begin the celebrations.

In the heat of the moment, it's easy for a buyer to make such a promise which he later regrets (probably because he had other appointments that day and unexpectedly found a more suitable home).

So, how will you know whether viewers are genuinely

interested in your home? Regardless of what is said, you probably won't. Often, the viewers who appeared least promising may buy the property, and those you thought were sure-fire purchasers fade away without ever making a decision. Therefore, everyone who comes through the door must be treated as a potential purchaser. The only way to gauge their interest is if they make an offer! Otherwise the agent can call them within a day and ask for their thoughts. Obtaining this feedback will help assess how the property is faring in the market. Your estate agent can then use the results to:

- Guide you on progress being made.

- Implement any changes necessary to increase the prospects of securing a buyer.

So It Won't Sell

Questions to be put to the agent, when reviewing how well the marketing of the property is going, include:

- What did the viewers think of the property? Did they criticize anything that could be rectified easily?

- If a number of appointments were not kept, why?

- This could be because the property was difficult to find and better directions are needed (or a 'For Sale' board to help locate it). Could the exterior be discouraging potential buyers from viewing internally; for example, is there an overgrown front garden or great difficulty in parking?

- Has the asking price deterred the public? If so, is it because the property market is generally quiet or has the price proved too optimistic? This is a question to ask after 4–6 weeks of marketing.

- How many times was the property advertised in the local newspapers and what response did this bring? If poor, does the advertisement need to be written in a more 'enticing' way? Would a newspaper with a different circulation help? Perhaps better photographs are needed.

- How is the property market faring? Is it just your home that is failing to sell, or is the market generally slow?

Armed with this information, a more informed decision can be made about the future marketing of the property. We would suggest reviewing the marketing every 3–4 weeks.

LOWER THE PRICE?

If after several weeks the property remains unsold, this is not necessarily a major problem. It might only call for a few tweaks to resolve matters. The agent should be able to guide you, based on the above questions. The most obvious remedy, however, and often the most 'painful', is reviewing the price. Has this proved too high? If based on the agent's recommendation, why has the figure proved unpopular? Demand specific answers.

If a price reduction is appropriate, then the alteration should be handled with care. Its purpose is to attract a new group of people with different aspirations. Reducing an asking price from £130,000 to £129,000 will not achieve this. Alter it to between £120,000 and £125,000 and this may introduce it to a new selection of potential purchasers and breathe life into the marketing.

The Last Resort

If the property remains unsold at the end of the agent's contract period, here are five options:

- Terminate your business with the present agent, observing any period of notice, and choose another. Sometimes even an agent who provides a good service can struggle to sell a particular property. Once placed in the hands of another company, things can suddenly 'click' and a buyer is found.

- Approach the other agents who first valued your home. Ask for advice on resolving matters. Expect specific solutions rather than vague promises.

- Continue with the present agency if you have faith in their eventually finding a buyer.

- *Multiple agency.* If you wish to remain with your present agent, but increase your options, instruct two or more agents. However, we have always felt that this alternative smacks of desperation and sends out the wrong signals to potential buyers. If a property remains unsold, then the difficulty is probably more fundamental than just the number of agents selling it. Instead, the root of the problem needs to be examined; for example, price, condition, state of the property market, etc.

- Choose another method of marketing while still using the services of an estate agent. Try selling privately using local newspapers, websites and a private 'For Sale' board. However, ensure any contract with your estate agent makes it clear that if you succeed in selling the property, you don't pay the agent any commission on the sale.

9

THE OFFER

In time, a potential buyer will appear. This is an exciting moment, as it brings us a step closer to the goal of selling our property. However, it is important not to be swept along by the momentum and overlook the offer process which is vital to ensuring success. This is the first test of how well we have chosen our estate agent. When considering an offer, the role of the agent is fundamental. He must:

• Ask the right questions of potential buyers.

• Use his expertise to interpret their responses correctly.

The way this is tackled will directly influence the quality of the sale. A disorganized and haphazard method will increase the chance of problems occurring, whereas a more methodical approach will diminish the danger of unexpected snags.

We hope that it is now becoming clear why so much effort was spent choosing the right estate agent. His knowledge and experience will now be used to guide us through the offer process, by accumulating as much relevant information about our prospective buyer as he can, in order to:

- Help us to make an informed decision about the buyer.

- Continue to use this information to bring our sale to a successful conclusion.

The offer stage, therefore, is really where the estate agent's job begins in earnest.

The Offer Form

What is our goal when someone makes us an offer? Obviously, we want to know how much he's willing to pay, although this is only half the story. Would you buy a can of paint without knowing its colour? Of course not. You'd want more information about the contents. The same applies when deciding if an offer is suitable. We need further details about the circumstances surrounding it.

1. Who is buying the property?
We need to be in no doubt about exactly who the purchaser is.

2. Have all interested parties seen the property?
It is vital to confirm that all parties involved with the purchase have viewed your home. Never rely on an offer given on someone else's behalf, except where they have written authority. For example, it is unsatisfactory for a couple to offer when only one of them has seen the property. Assurances may be given that a decision can be made on the other's behalf, but if you agree a sale on this basis you run the serious risk of the absent partner visiting your home later and deciding against it.

3. The Offer
Regarding the offer itself, it is quite likely that the agent may need further guidance from you on a few points:

- Can the agent divulge to the potential buyer what price would be acceptable to you? This is useful if the property has been marketed for many months without success, and you are keen to sell.

• Can he have written authority to refuse an offer below a certain level?

• Should the agent 'play hardball' and explain to all interested parties that you want 'close to the asking price?' This may be preferable if the property is new to the market.

• Can the agent suggest to potential buyers that there may be some flexibility in the asking price?

4. Is a mortgage necessary?

This is as important as the offer figure itself. With the buyer's permission, knowing his financial arrangements is the only way of really confirming his suitability as a purchaser.

If a mortgage is required, details of the mortgage lender or financial adviser are taken. Information about the deposit is also useful, such as:

• If in a savings account, is there a period of notice before the money can be withdrawn?

• If abroad, how long will it take to transfer it to the UK?

• Is it being borrowed from family and friends, and are they fully committed to this?

Most people are happy to supply such information, believing it will give their offer more credence. Those who refuse normally have a reason and we must question what this is.

Finally, if there is resistance to disclosing information regarding the deposit (or if your buyer is wholly 'cash'), then the agent might ask that the buyer's solicitor confirms the buyer's financial situation to your solicitor. If the buyer still refuses, then ask yourself why. Do you really want to do business without verifying such important information?

5. *Timescale*

To help clarify how long the sale may take to complete, find out from the buyer:

- When does he want to move?

- Is he using a mortgage scheme which expires by a certain date?

- Is a holiday booked which could delay the sale?

- Will the purchaser wait if the owner intends to buy another property, and has yet to find one?

6. *Property to Sell?*

If the applicant has a property to sell, or it's under offer, details are needed of the estate agent involved (or of the solicitor, if the sale is a private one). Should the prospective purchaser have no property to sell, then he will fall into one of the following categories:

- First-time buyer.

- Cash buyer. The purchaser has no property to sell and does not need a loan.

- Nothing to sell. This party may own a property but will not need to sell it in order to buy yours (he may still need a mortgage). It is useful to know what he intends to do with his present home. If he plans to rent it out, for example, will he need to find a tenant before the finance company offers him a new mortgage?

Why all the Questions?

You may be surprised by the number of questions that need to be asked. Why isn't it enough to take an offer from a prospective purchaser and trust the information he gives us?

In an ideal world, it would be wonderful to be given a figure, enter into a little friendly haggling, and then settle on a satisfactory price with a shake of the hands. This approach might have been possible years ago, when business was conducted in a more civilized fashion, but follow this route today and it is an almost certain recipe for disaster and heartache. We have all heard horror stories about purchasers suddenly finding themselves short of money on the day of exchange, or unable to obtain a mortgage which they were promised was just a formality. We experienced this at our estate agency more times than we care to remember.

The sad truth is that people sometimes say things that are untrue or incorrect simply because they have been poorly advised, do not understand the system or because agents don't ask the right questions. Take the example of people who explain that they are 'cash buyers' or that their property is 'sold'. These two terms can mean different things to different people.

- Does 'sold' mean that they have found a buyer for their home or that they have already completed the transaction and moved out?

- Does 'cash' imply that they have the necessary money to buy your home, or that shares need to be sold (which may fall dramatically in value)?

We even met people who believed that they were cash buyers although they required a mortgage. It's all a matter of interpretation. Under certain circumstances, it could also be suggested that a minority seek to bend the truth when making an offer, to strengthen their position. Only by questioning a

buyer can we hope to discover the truth and prevent setting in
motion a sale which is doomed to failure.

Evaluating the Offer
With the offer stage over, and the right questions asked, it is
time to judge the suitability of our applicants. There are two
considerations:

• Are the circumstances surrounding the offer satisfactory?

• Is the figure offered acceptable?

Finance
If your buyer requires a mortgage, he will use either an
independent financial adviser or a bank/building society. If the
former, then your estate agent will want to speak with him and
confirm the mortgage details. This will not be possible with
the latter as these institutions refuse to talk to third parties.
Questions asked include:

• In the adviser's opinion, can the applicant achieve the
  amount of mortgage needed?

• When will the survey be undertaken?

• How long will it take for the mortgage to be issued?

• Are there any matters that might cause a delay?

• If the property requires a large amount of modernization,
  have the purchasers allowed for this in their mortgage
  calculations? (This is also a good question for the
  purchaser.)

It is possible that your estate agents provide mortgage services,
allowing them to discover first hand the financial background

of your buyer and play a leading role in this matter (within the bounds of the Data Protection Act).

Those buyers who are 'cash' should be asked if confirmation of this is possible, by providing a bank statement or asking the applicant's solicitors to confirm to your solicitor that the cash is available, in the UK, and with no delay.

Selling Position

If the buyer has no property to sell, then he is worth his weight in gold. We are reliant only on him to buy our home, rather than numerous others in a chain. The word chain is used to describe the situation where one homeowner is selling to another, who in turn is selling to another, etc., until the final buyer has no property to sell and the chain is complete.

However, if the buyer does have a property to sell, be wary of agreeing a sale until he has secured a purchaser.

If he has already done this, your agent will contact the buyer's estate agent to make enquiries about his own buyer. He will discover:

- When the sale was agreed. If some time ago, is the buyer still proceeding?

- Whether the buyer's financial arrangements are satisfactory.

- If the legal work is in hand.

If your purchaser's purchaser has a property to sell, and, if so, what the details are surrounding the rest of the chain.

The Price

An applicant's first offer on your home is seldom his last; he is probably expecting to increase it. The success of these negotiations will depend on the agent's skill. Avoid protracted negotiations over many weeks as frustration normally sets in, and the chance of finding common ground diminishes. If a satisfactory figure cannot be agreed on, leave the 'door open' for the future. Suggest that if he decides at a later date to increase his figure, you'll be happy to discuss it (but make sure this conversation ends with the phrase 'if the property is still available!').

There are occasions where an offer is far from a homeowner's expectations. However, it may still be worthy of consideration if:

• The property has remained unsold after many months. Perhaps it has now found its true price level; a property is only worth as much as someone is willing to pay for it.

• The asking price was optimistic, and lower offers were expected.

Multiple Offers
If there are several offers on your home, you have the option of:

• Choosing one that is superior to the rest.

• Asking the agent to return to each party and ask for their 'best and final bid' within 48 hours. This gives everyone the opportunity to increase their offer, produces a quick answer, and injects a sense of competition into the proceedings, which should help achieve the highest figure possible.

• Allowing two or more buyers to proceed, on the understanding that the first to produce a satisfactory mortgage offer will be given the chance to buy the property. A variation of this is called a 'contract race'. It works on a similar principle; every interested party proceeds with the purchase, and the first to exchange contracts secures the property. However, we must add that while these options are viable, we dislike them and feel that they are generally an unfair way to conduct business.

• Agreeing a sale with one party but on a strict timescale; for example, he has four weeks to exchange contracts. If he is unsuccessful, then there is still the possibility of the other interested parties being available.

• Asking the agent why so many bids have appeared, especially if the property has only just come to the market. It could just be a fortunate situation, which we need to take full advantage of, or maybe something has gone awry with the asking price, which perhaps should have been higher. If this is the case, it is an unpleasant situation to be in, and one which is challenging to resolve. You can either:

– Refuse all bids. Increase the asking price of the property, and start the marketing again. If doing this, it may be better to remove the property from the market for a month before remarketing, as the buying public may have already associated your home with a particular price. When a few weeks have elapsed, marketing can begin anew, hopefully appealing to new buyers who were not aware of the previous price. You may also want to change your estate agent if you have lost faith in the present company you are using. However, check the contract first as you may be committed to the agency for a certain length of time, or the agency may need to be given a period of notice before the contract is terminated.

– Negotiate. It is possible that the parties currently interested may be prepared to pay more than the asking price. If they are keen to buy, and aware that others are also interested, then asking each party for the best bid by a certain date may help to achieve a more realistic figure.

Finally, it must be made clear that the most active time for a property new to the market is the first few weeks. Therefore, it is certainly not impossible that offers will appear during this period. Often, homeowners refuse early offers at perfectly reasonable prices, only to discover that very few more offers materialize once the initial flurry of activity begins to wane. This is not to suggest that the first offer should be accepted, or the property should not be fully marketed; far from it. We must understand how these things work and stay aware of all possibilities. If you have chosen your estate agent wisely, using the criteria discussed previously, then he will be able to advise you and resolve matters in your favour.

Agreeing a Sale

Once matters have been finalized and it is time to agree a sale there is one final question the homeowner needs to ask himself:

• Do you propose to sell your home and buy another, or simply move out regardless?

If the latter, then the situation is simple; proceed immediately with the sale. If, though, you need to find a property to buy, then the proposed purchaser should be told. If he is content to wait, then, again, agree the sale; this will put you in a stronger bargaining position when property hunting (but don't spend any money on the sale until you find a property to buy).

10

AFTER THE SALE IS AGREED

If you had chosen a mediocre estate agent, his job would now be finished. A buyer has been found, a sale has been agreed and it is simply a matter of him waiting for his commission to roll in. But luckily, we chose an above average agent. This agent will appreciate that his knowledge and experience is about to be put to the test.

Once an offer has been agreed, there is little for the owner to do. The majority of work is now in the hands of others: solicitors, estate agents, the purchaser and the mortgage lender. There is no standard timetable when selling property. It can take four weeks or six months. It depends on a variety of factors such as the length of the chain, the time taken to obtain a mortgage, or complete the legal paperwork, the results of the EPC, the desire of purchaser and owner, etc.

As a brief guide to the processes involved, this chapter presents an example of the activities which need to be undertaken during a three month sale. The first eight weeks involve preparing for an exchange of contracts (after which point both buyer and seller are legally bound), and then a further four weeks until completion (when the buyer finally takes ownership of the property).

WEEK 1

LETTERS

Immediately after the sale is agreed, your estate agent will send out a letter called the 'Memorandum of Sale'. This contains details of the parties involved in the sale, and the price agreed. Four copies of the Memorandum of Sale are sent out, one to the purchaser, one to the homeowner, and one to each of their solicitors.

MORTGAGE FORMS

If your purchaser needs a mortgage, he will complete the necessary forms and usually pay for the survey, although occasionally a mortgage lender will offer a free survey. The mortgage lender may require additional paperwork from the purchaser; for example, confirmation of pay, identification, credit check, etc.

LEGAL WORK

If this has not been prepared, the homeowner now needs to instruct his solicitor to begin the legal process. This includes:

• Preparing a contract. As discussed on page 79, the title deeds have become redundant in favour of the new Title Information Document issued by the Land Registry. From this document, a contract is created for the purchaser's solicitor, which details conditions affecting the sale. It is important that all relevant title documents are sent to avoid delays.

• 'Seller's Property Information Form'. Completed by the owner, this document covers topics such as the property's boundaries, disputes with neighbours, alterations to the property, and available services, for example, gas and electricity. Owners of leasehold property complete a second form dealing with their lease and outgoing costs.

- Energy Performance Certificate.

- Fixtures and fittings list. This details items to be left at the property.

VERIFYING THE SALE
A few days after the agent sends the Memorandum of Sale, he will confirm that:

- The purchaser's financial matters have been arranged, and he has instructed his solicitor to begin working on the legal documents when received.

- The searches have been paid for and have been put in hand.

- Any chain associated with the sale is equally well advanced. Rather than relying on second-hand information, ask your agent to speak directly to all the agents in the chain. There is no substitute for hearing things 'straight from the horse's mouth'.

WEEK 2
If the agent believes that anyone needs to be reminded again to organize any of the above, then this is the week to do it. Alternatively, it might be decided to let everyone have the chance to organize themselves without any pressure from the agent.

WEEK 3
SURVEY
After 7–21 days, a period which varies according to how busy the property market is, the buyer's mortgage lender will survey the property. This is arranged via the estate agent. There may be more than one survey, depending on the type chosen by the purchaser.

Little preparation is required before the surveyor arrives. Surveyors are trained to see beneath the veneer, and disregard children's toys on the floor, or clothes strewn over the bedroom. It is not necessary for the owner to be at home, although the surveyor may want to ask questions or gain access to areas of the property with the owner's help; for example, the loft, basement, outhouses, etc. Lastly, don't expect the surveyor to divulge the contents of his report.

CHECK PROGRESS
The agent should once again check your buyer's progress and that of the chain. If any party appears slow, then it is important to know why. Have all the surveys taken place in the chain? How is the legal work proceeding? This should then be reported back to the homeowner.

LEGAL WORK
How far has your own legal work progressed? The two solicitors should be well under way. If a flat is being sold, are any documents needed from the company dealing with the running of the block? Having received your solicitor's legal documents, the purchaser's solicitor may have further questions, which are called 'Additional Enquiries'.

WEEK 4
This is an ideal opportunity for the homeowner and estate agent to liaise and review how the sale is progressing. Look at what has been achieved, and what is expected in the next few weeks.

WEEK 5–6
HOMEOWNER'S POSITION
If the owner is moving without buying another property, is rented accommodation needed? With the sale so far progressed, now is the time to start making enquiries about renting accommodation in anticipation of a successful sale (although it is still too early to give any definite commitment).

CHECK THE SALE
Your estate agent now asks:

- Whether the purchaser's mortgage has been issued and are there any conditions associated with it. For example, is it subject to additional paperwork or further inspection of the property?

- Is the survey satisfactory? If matters have arisen, then this is the time to try and resolve them. This might include the need for additional surveys to ascertain the cost for such defects as damp or woodworm.

- Are there any legal matters outstanding? Can the agent help to quicken the process? It is surprising what a skilled and experienced estate agent can organize!

- Is the rest of the chain as well progressed as we are?

WEEK 6–7
With the target of an 8 week exchange looming ever closer, week 6/7 is used to contact the buyer, financial adviser, and chain to confirm their progress once more.

- The buyer will need to have his deposit arranged by now.

- Any outstanding legal matters need to be reported back to the homeowner.

- Any delays in the chain need to be questioned and resolved.

- Have the searches been returned? (See page 59.) These are often left by the buyer's solicitors until most other matters have been satisfactorily resolved, in order to save the client's money should problems have occurred earlier in the sale.

WEEK 7
PREPARE FOR EXCHANGE
Before 'exchange of contracts', the following points need to be completed throughout the chain:

- All buyers have satisfactory mortgages.

- All legal work is completed, including searches.

- The buyers are arranging for their deposits to be given to the appropriate solicitors. These should be in the form of banker's drafts or building society cheques, and time should be allowed for them to clear. (If using a personal cheque, it must be ensured that this would be acceptable!) It is possible that using a particular legal mechanism, each buyer will be relying on using the deposit of the buyer beneath him in the chain, via the solicitors.

- Completion date agreed.

When all is ready, the solicitor will ask the seller to visit his office, read the contract and ask any questions. (The post can be used, but a meeting is far better for such an important event.) The contract is then signed. This, however, does not yet mean the property is sold. That requires an 'exchange of contracts'.

WEEK 8
THE EXCHANGE
The exchange of contracts is the 'point of no return' in a sale. At this point, the owner becomes legally bound to sell his home to the purchaser who, in turn, is legally bound to buy it. However, there is still a remote possibility of the latter withdrawing from the sale, although the penalties are so severe that this is a very rare occurrence.

Considering how significant this stage is, the actual procedure involved is quite mundane. It takes place over the phone, and between the solicitors. We have outlined the procedure on page 71. Once finished, the homeowner can plan for his moving day, knowing that he has just one final hurdle before he has successfully sold his home: the day of completion.

THE PROBLEM CLINIC
RESOLVING PROBLEMS
Horror stories abound of problems that occur during property sales. However, approached in the right way, so many of them are resolvable. Below are some of the more common ones we have confronted over the years.

1. PRICE REDUCTION
A common problem for homeowners is being asked for a price reduction after a survey. It can be a testing time, but handled in the correct way, and with a skilful estate agent, stress levels can be kept to a minimum.

Firstly, decide if the request is legitimate. If due to a defect highlighted in a separate survey, ask to see the relevant portion of the report. If this is refused, then start to 'smell a rat'. Without proof, how can you be expected to give a reduction? If, having seen the report, however, it is a problem that could not have been foreseen, then it is reasonable for the purchaser to expect this to be reflected in the price, for example, discovering damp or woodworm. The purchaser should organize a specialist company or firm to visit and quote for the repairs. Armed with their estimate, the homeowner will then decide whether to agree to a reduction. Two points are worth considering:

• If the homeowner refuses, and the buyer withdraws, then the same issues are likely to recur with the next purchaser. Surely it's better to confront them now?

- If the amount is relatively small (i.e. £500–£1,000), is it worth losing the sale for? That much has probably already been spent in time, effort, and possibly legal expenses.

When considering any reduction, always ask to see the final pages of the survey report. These are normally where the surveyor gives his overall impression of the property, and an opinion on the price. If this figure is the same as the one being paid by the purchaser, then plainly the surveyor believes that this is the correct price, even allowing for any repairs.

There are circumstances where the request for a price reduction is unreasonable.

- The purchaser suddenly realizes that the bedrooms are smaller than he remembered.

- The purchaser wants to extend the property in the future, and believes the owner should make a contribution.

- The survey described the kitchen as dated – something blindingly obvious to anyone who visited the property.

These might seem to be ridiculous examples but we have dealt with them all over the years, and they only prove that buying and selling property brings out the worst in people. In these situations the homeowner must decide:

- How much is it worth keeping the buyer?

- Can another 'more reasonable' buyer be found quickly?

- Is the buyer still serious about buying or really just trying to find an excuse to withdraw?

> *One of the most difficult sales we dealt with involved selling a substantial detached house, for a substantial amount of money to a party who on the day of exchange of contracts decided to withdraw because he discovered that the seller was going to remove shelving from the garage, worth £20!*
>
> *Fortunately, reason prevailed but it highlights how, in the pressurized circumstances that some buyers and sellers find themselves, they can often do the most illogical things.*

2. CHAIN BREAK

One of the disadvantages of a sale with a chain is that a successful outcome is reliant upon so many people. It only takes one party to fall by the wayside, and every other sale in the chain collapses. This can occur for a variety of reasons, most of which are out of our control, except one.

Imagine we are selling our home and buying another. There is a chain (see diagram overleaf).

We have sold 40 Station Road to Mr and Mrs X, who in turn are selling their flat to a first-time buyer. We are buying Miss W's house at 90 The Croft, who is moving to Rose Cottage. This is owned by Mr and Mrs P who are purchasing Mr J's home 'The Manor House'. Mr J is at the end of the chain, and will not be buying a property, as he has got another one already.

Unfortunately, Miss W's survey on Rose Cottage has not been good. It highlighted some costly matters that need attention (£6,000), which Miss W had not expected, and cannot afford. She asks for this amount to be reduced from the agreed price of £725,000. The owners refuse. A stalemate is reached. Neither party will back down and it looks as if the chain will collapse for the sake of this £6,000. Where can the money be found?

Owner	Property	Agreed Offer
Mr J	The Manor House ↑	£975,000
Mr and Mrs P	Rose Cottage ↑	£725,000
Miss W	90 The Croft ↑	£350,000
Us	40 Station Road ↑	£200,000
Mr and Mrs X	Flat 5, College Road	£120,000
Mr First-Time Buyer		

The answer is: from every other party in the chain. It is in everyone's interest to try and resolve this matter. Each party has already spent much money, time, and energy on their respective transactions, which will be wasted if the sales do not proceed. The skill of the estate agents will be needed here. They approach each party in the chain and ask for a contribution towards the £6,000 shortfall. This money can be 'passed' along the chain to Miss W by altering the agreed prices of each property. For example, the First-Time Buyer may agree to pay £500 more for Flat 5, Mr and Mrs X agree to pay an extra £500 more (i.e. an extra £1,000 in total) for 40 Station Road, and we too agree to pay an additional £500 more for Miss W's The Croft. This now gives Miss W an extra £1,500 that she did not have before. If Mr J at the top of the chain reduces the price of his home by £2,000, Mr and Mrs P can also pass this saving to Miss W. She now has £3,500 towards the £6,000 needed.

The next stage involves the estate agents. They need to reduce their commission fee to each party by £500. This too would be passed to Miss W by altering the price of each property again to allow for the fact that each party is now paying £500 less in estate agent's commission, which can be factored into the price of each home. As there are five agents involved, this brings us in another £2,500. Our goal of 'giving' Miss W £6,000 is achieved, at only a minimal cost to each party. Now the sale can go ahead.

This may seem an extreme example. With the price of the property Miss W is buying, would she really let the sale fall through for the sake of £6,000? We have seen it happen, and for a lot less money. 'Principle' and 'ego' can cloud people's judgments. With the cool-headedness of the others in the chain, though, these situations can often be successfully resolved. It just needs all parties to 'pull in the same direction'.

3. No Survey
If, four weeks after agreeing a sale, there is no survey by the purchaser, then questions need to be asked by your estate agent.

* Has the survey been paid for? If not, then why not?

* If the purchaser has not yet settled on a mortgage lender, then it is time this decision was made!

* If the mortgage lender will not arrange a survey until certain documents have been received, can these be chased? (These documents may include wage references, past credit history, confirmation of identification, etc.)

* Have issues surfaced that concern the mortgage lender and so have delayed them arranging a survey?

This is a good example of why keeping a property on the market, even after agreeing a sale, is preferable. Other potential buyers can be found in case the present buyer proves too slow at, or incapable of, obtaining a mortgage.

4. No Mortgage Offer

After survey, mortgage offers should appear a week or so later. Much depends on the lender, but if after 2–3 weeks an offer has not materialized, then the agent needs to discover:

- Has the lender received all of the necessary documents in order to issue a mortgage? If not, what is missing? The agent or financial adviser should chase these immediately.

- Is the postal service to blame? If so, then can a duplicate offer be sent?

- Has a problem occurred that stops the lender from making the offer? Can the problem be resolved or will a new buyer need to be secured?

5. Slow Solicitors

If the purchaser's solicitor is slow in dealing with the legal paperwork, is there a reason? While it could be because of a heavy workload, it may also be on the instructions of the purchaser. The question is why – does the buyer have a problem or some hidden agenda? Has he even instructed his solicitor to start the process, and paid him the necessary funds? This is a matter for the estate agent to investigate.

6. Purchasers Failing to Respond to Phone Calls

On the occasions we had a sale fall through, it often started with purchasers failing to return phone calls. If a problem occurs, some purchasers follow the 'ostrich principle' and bury their heads in the sand. They refuse to discuss the matter with anyone, deciding instead to ignore all contact, even with their own solicitor. If a letter from the estate agent asking for a reply in five days also produces no results, then presume the worst and start looking for other buyers immediately.

7. SLOW PURCHASERS

Dealing with some purchasers can be like pulling teeth. Not only are they slow in moving the process along, they need to be constantly pushed to complete every necessary task. Working on the 'Jager' principle that there is a 'reason for everything', this could be due to some concern about the purchase. If, after agreeing a sale, the purchaser is still undecided about your home, he may slow the process, hoping to find a more suitable property to buy. He may even have placed offers on several homes and is still unsure about which to pursue.

Imagine the situation of a buyer who, after agreeing a sale, takes two weeks to find a solicitor, and another two agreeing a suitable mortgage. He then takes yet another week to instruct the solicitor to proceed, and fourteen more days to pay for a survey. This is not a buyer with serious intentions. In this situation, the homeowner would definitely keep his property on the market, hoping to find a more committed buyer.

8. SLOW TO EXCHANGE

For most, reaching the exchange of contracts cannot come quickly enough. But occasionally, as this time approaches, a purchaser will suddenly announce that he cannot arrange to see his solicitor to sign the contract. Work or family commitments are common excuses. Working on the principle that there is a 'reason for everything', alarm bells should start ringing.

Ask the estate agent to confirm with the solicitor that the legal work and the mortgage offer have been arranged. Anything outstanding must be investigated immediately. This may hold the key to the purchaser's reluctance to proceed. Perhaps, for example, the mortgage offer has not yet been issued although it was promised weeks ago. Could this suggest a problem that neither you nor your estate agent were aware of? Could there be a problem with the purchaser's deposit? The agent will need to use his skills to ask the appropriate questions and unearth the truth.

PART THREE

BUYING AND SELLING PROPERTY: THE FINAL STEP

11

FROM EXCHANGE TO COMPLETION

One of the busiest times during a sale, for both buyer and seller, is the period between 'exchange' (exchange of contracts) and 'completion' (the moment when a purchaser takes ownership). At this point the balance of the purchase price is transferred to the seller, via solicitors.

There is much to organize and, because most of the tasks are common to both parties, this chapter has been written with both in mind.

After Exchange
Although the estate agent's job is almost finished after exchange, there remains much for solicitor, buyer and seller to do. While the solicitor has further paperwork to complete, the buyer and seller will be preparing for a smooth move, by informing people of the big event.

WHOM TO TELL?
Who needs to know about your impending move?

- Telephone company. Sellers should ask for the phone to be disconnected on the day of the move (and have alternative means of contact for when completion takes place). Purchasers should inform the telephone company in good time if they wish to continue with the connection.

- Utility companies (gas, electricity, water and drainage).

- Friends and family.

- Milkman and newspaper shop.

- Royal Mail. If post is to be redirected, there are forms to be completed. However, buyers need to check regularly with the sellers that post has not mistakenly been sent to their new address, prior to completion; for example, mortgage or insurance documents.

- Council tax.

- Doctor and dentist (signing on with new ones if necessary).

- DVLA (driving licences and car registration).

- Credit card companies, banks, etc.

- Authorities regarding television licences, gun certificates, etc.

- Mobile phone companies.

- Companies with whom you hold a pension, savings, shares, investments, etc.

- Any providers of purchases already booked, for example, holidays.

THE SOLICITOR'S ROLE
Purchaser's Solicitor
Legal documents required after 'exchange' include:

- *Bankruptcy Search* – this confirms that the person receiving the mortgage is not a bankrupt.

- *Final Land Registry Search*.

- *Requisitions on Title*. This form confirms such matters as:

  – The property will be sold empty (i.e. all parties having vacated).

  – Keys will be available.

  – Confirmation that the owner's mortgage will be redeemed on completion.

  – How final payment is to be made for the property.

  – How other legal documents needed for completion will be made available.

A request will be made for mortgage monies to be released before the day of completion.

Owner's Solicitor
The document that transfers ownership to the purchaser on completion is signed by the seller.

Both solicitors will also provide a 'Completion Statement' outlining all costs involved with the conveyancing, and requesting the buyer to pay all the remaining funds, including stamp duty land tax the day before completion.

THE MOVING DAY

On the day of completion, once the seller has vacated the property, it is usual for his keys to be left with the estate agent. (Those purchasing a property privately will need to arrange collection direct.) These are given to the purchaser immediately after completion has taken place. When the owner's solicitor has received the buyer's money, he will ring the estate agent and instruct him to release the keys. At this point, the seller vacates, and the buyer can move in.

Because the actual transfer of money is in the hands of others, completion can happen at almost any time during the completion day. It is possible for a purchaser to be packed and ready to move, but waiting hours for access to the new home. What can be done to quicken and smooth the process? Confirm with the mortgage lender and solicitor a few days beforehand that they are fully prepared for completion and nothing is outstanding. This should avert any last-minute surprises. It is important to try to organize all funds the day before, as one of the most common reasons for delays on completion day is waiting for funds to be sent by either the buyer or their lender. Regardless of the actual time of completion, it is the seller's responsibility to be ready to vacate as soon as possible on the day. If completion takes place at 12.30 pm, but the owners are still packing at 4.30 pm, the purchasers will not be impressed. A good standard time by which completion usually should have taken place is 2 pm; by then the seller should have vacated and the money should have been received by his solicitor. That means that nobody is moving into their home with daylight fading, and the prospect of unpacking late into the night. This is also a good reason for the seller to use a professional removal company, who is quick and efficient, rather than attempting the job himself.

If possible, the buyer should ask to inspect the property before completion. Although this may be disruptive to the owners, it is an ideal time to confirm that:

- The property will be left clean and tidy.

- The agreed fixtures and fittings are there.

- The utility meters have been read, to ensure that the correct amount is charged to each party i.e. gas, electricity, water, etc. It is best if both the buyer and seller take their own readings.

After Completion

The buyer needs to:

- Make the stamp duty payment to the solicitor.

- Ensure that the solicitor registers the property in the buyer's name.

- Send the title information document to the mortgage lender for safe keeping

APPENDIX ONE

WHEN BUYING AND SELLING GOES BAD!

However well we might have planned the buying or selling of a property, there is always the potential for problems to occur. While these might be due to the inadequate property system in this country, occasionally it may involve the companies or firms we deal with.

Unhappy with the treatment from a solicitor?

Dissatisfied with the actions of an estate agent?

Your first port of call for any problem is with the owner, manager or senior partner. It may be a matter that can be resolved by him, with the minimum of fuss. However, if this doesn't help, then the following organizations may be able to offer guidance (if the offending company is one of its members):

National Federation of Property Professionals
National Association of Estate Agents
Arbon House
6 Tournament Court
Edgehill Drive
Warwick
CV34 6LG
Tel: 0844 387 0555
www.naea.co.uk

The Property Ombudsman (TPO)

This is an independent body that offers recourse to those unhappy with their treatment from an estate agent. It has the power to fine and can deal with such matters as breach of law, poor quality of service, and a range of other disputes that may arise. The maximum that the TPO can award is £25,000.

The Property Ombudsman
Beckett House
4 Bridge Street
Salisbury
Wiltshire
SP1 2LX
Tel: 01722 333306
Email: admin@tpos.co.uk
www.tpos.co.uk

Ombudsman Services: Property (OSP)

This is also an independent body, which will aim to sort out a complaint with a property company; 'Property companies' include chartered surveyors, surveyors, estate agents, residential managing or letting agents and valuers. The Ombudsman Services is appointed by the Royal Institution of Chartered

Surveyors (RICS) and the Association of Residential Managing Agents (ARMA) to handle any complaints about their members. The same guidelines must be followed as for those agents who are a member of The Property Ombudsman and the maximum award is also £25,000.

Ombudsman Services: Property
PO Box 10
Warrington
WA4 9FE
Tel: 0330 440 1634
Textphone: 0330 440 11600

It is now a legal requirement that an estate agency has to belong to either The Property Ombudsman – TPO, or the Ombudsmen Services: Property – OSP.

Office of Fair Trading (Trading Standards)
Fleetbank House
2–6 Salisbury Square
London
EC4Y 8JX
www.oft.gov.uk

The Law Society
Solicitors Regulation Authority
Ipsley Court
Berrington Close
Redditch
B98 0TD
Tel: 0870 606 2555
www.lawsociety.org.uk

Royal Institute of Chartered Surveyors
RICS Contact Centre
Surveyor Court
Westwood Way
Coventry
CV4 8JE
Tel: 0870 3331600
www.rics.org

APPENDIX TWO

GLOSSARY OF TERMS

Applicant   Party wishing to buy a property. Also called a buyer.

Broker   Another term for a financial adviser, i.e. an individual who organizes mortgages.

Buyer   Party purchasing a property.

Chain   Where a homeowner buys a property from a party who in turn is purchasing another property, this is a chain. It can be many properties long.

Commission fee   Fee charged by an estate agent to the homeowner for selling a home.

Commonhold   Another method of legally owning property in addition to freehold and leasehold. It is a variation of freehold, where several properties can share a single freehold, i.e. each apartment in a block of flats can have its own share of the building's freehold. Therefore it dispenses with the disadvantage of having a lease, which is an ever wasting asset, and the need for an external landlord.

Completion

The end of the buying process and the moment when a purchaser takes ownership of a property (is given the keys and normally moves in).

Contract

A legal document signed by both buyer and seller, prior to exchange of contracts, details information about the property being bought, and is a legal commitment that the buyer will buy, and that the seller will sell, on the completion day.

Conveyance

The transfer of ownership of property or land from one party to another.

Covenant

A restriction imposed on land or property (for example, not being allowed to use your home as business premises, or being restricted from converting a house into apartments).

Deposit

The money needed by a purchaser to bridge the gap between the price of a property and the amount of the mortgage. The deposit can also refer to the 10 per cent which the buyer puts down on exchange of contracts (no connection with any mortgage).

Easement

An entitlement to rights over someone else's land (for example, right of way).

Exchange

The moment when a purchaser is legally committed to buy a property and the homeowner is legally committed to sell it.

Financial adviser

A party who arranges mortgages.

Fixtures and fittings

Items which remain at the property when it has been sold. Fixtures are immoveable items such as kitchen cupboards or a fireplace; fittings are moveable items such as carpets, curtains and light fittings.

Flat

A property, often one of several properties in a block reached via a communal entrance.

Freehold

A method of owning land in England and Wales.

Freeholder

Owner of a block of flats, or indeed of any other freehold property.

Gazump

A higher offer being accepted on a property, although a sale is already proceeding.

Gazunder

When the buyer demands a reduction in price having already had his offer accepted (but before exchange of contracts).

Ground rent   A charge paid by flat and maisonette owners to the freeholder.

Joint sole agency   Two different estate agents, working together to sell a property and dividing the fee between them.

Lease   For the purpose of this book, this term describes a document which, among other things, details the responsibilities of each property owner in a block of flats or maisonettes, and specifies the length of the lease and the charges. However, the term 'lease' is also the name of a document concerned with the rental of commercial and residential properties.

Leasehold   One way of legally owning land in England and Wales. It is the exclusive possession of a property for an agreed period of time.

Maintenance charge   See service charge.

Maisonette   Similar to a flat except that it usually has its own front door, rather than a communal entrance.

Managing agent   A company employed to maintain a block of flats or maisonettes. It may be employed by the freeholder to collect service charges and ground rent, and organize the upkeep of the building.

Market appraisal

An estate agent visits a property and provides the homeowner with an asking price for the building. This is also called 'taking an instruction', or 'valuation'.

Mortgage

A loan secured on a property, normally used to buy it.

Multiple agency

Instructing more than one estate agent to market a property, but only the agent that sells it is paid.

New instruction

A property being marketed by an estate agent that has just become available.

Pulling out

Withdrawing from a purchase.

Purpose built

A building constructed for its actual purpose; for example, a block of flats. The opposite would be a conversion; for example, flats in what was originally a single house.

Requisitions on Title

Documents dealt with by solicitors between exchange and completion. Can include land registry and bankruptcy searches.

Residents' Association

A group formed by residents in a community or block of flats with responsibility for the upkeep.

Right of way

Access over someone else's land.

Service charge   An amount paid for maintenance of the building.

Sole agency   Instructing one agent to sell a property.

Stamp duty land tax   A tax paid to the government by the purchaser of a property. The amount paid is determined by the value of the building.

Subsidence   When a building or the ground beneath it sinks to a lower level, resulting in movement of the building and causing cracks to appear. Can be caused by failing foundations.

Survey   The inspection of a property by a surveyor. Depending on the type of survey chosen, it involves examining the structure of a building, its fittings and state of repair.

Surveyor   Person employed by mortgagee and/ or purchaser to look carefully at a property and advise on its condition, as well as confirming the building's suitability for a loan.

Title deeds   A document proving ownership of land or property.

Valuation (agent)   See market appraisal.

Valuation (survey)   Surveyor's opinion of property value provided on survey report.

Vendor   Party who owns a property for sale. Also known as the homeowner or seller.

Withdraw   A homeowner or purchaser who decides not to proceed with the sale (also termed 'pulling out').

INDEX

Also in Right Way

SUCCESSFUL PROPERTY LETTING

by David Lawrenson

Whether you are a new or experienced landlord, this bestselling and fully up-to-date book will show you how to buy the right property in the right location (including abroad) for high rents and capital growth.

- Get great property deals from developers and private sellers
- How to get the best from letting agents
- Comply with all the laws and avoid the tenants from hell
- Minimise your property tax bill

David Lawrenson has 25 years' experience as a landlord and property expert and runs a consultancy service at *www.LettingFocus.com* for landlords and organisations wishing to market to the private rented sector. His straight-talking views on property investment often appear in the media.

'It stands out as a practical and extremely detailed guide for landlords . . . crammed full of tips.'
National Landlords Association

'Excellent guidance . . . a valuable contribution to the savvy landlord's bookshelf.'
Landlordzone.co.uk

www.constablerobinson.com